Cunningham's
Book
of
Shadows

About This Book

The basis for this Book of Shadows is an unfinished manuscript Scott Cunningham started more than thirty years ago. The way it was placed in an envelope with the title shows us Scott intended it to be published.

We believe it would be a disservice to publish it in "the raw," and for that reason we have excerpted passages from Scott's previously published books to serve as introductions to sections or to create bridges where material was not completed. The primary resource was *Wicca: A Guide for the Solitary Practitioner*, and those passages are noted for clarity. None of Scott's original words were changed for this book.

The original manuscript was produced on a red IBM Selectric® typewriter, and many of those pages have been reproduced exactly as they were created, including Scott's handwritten notes and corrections in the margins. Also, many of the hand-drawn symbols and related artwork have been reproduced just as he drew them.

This is not a traditional Book of Shadows because Scott intended to create something truly unique. The genesis of that idea and the content of the book is explained in the "How to Use This Book" section written by Scott's publisher, Carl Llewellyn Weschcke.

The appendices contain memories of Scott from some of his siblings, teachers, and closest friends.

Scott Cunningham

Scott Cunningham learned about Wicca while still in high school, and practiced elemental magic for over twenty years. He was the author of more than forty books, both fiction and non-fiction, sixteen of them published by Llewellyn Publications. He experienced, researched, then wrote about what he learned in his magical training. Scott's books reflect a broad range of interests within the New Age sphere, where he was highly regarded. He passed from this life on March 28, 1993, after a long illness.

Cunningham's
Book
of
Shadows

The Path of an American Traditionalist

Scott Cunningham

Llewellyn Publications
Woodbury, Minnesota

First Edition
First Printing, 2009

Cover design by Kevin R. Brown
Editing by Connie Hill
Llewellyn is a registered trademark of Llewellyn Worldwide, Ltd.

Interior art work has been scanned in from the author's original manuscript.

Some of the prayers, chants, and invocations are traditional chants that are in common usage. Among them, the Witches Rune (p 69) is attributed to, among others, Stewart and Janet Farrar (*The Witches' Goddess*); the Call to Pan to Dion Fortune; and the Healing Invocation to Isis to an ancient papyrus.

Library of Congress Cataloging-in-Publication Data.
Cunningham, Scott, 1956–1993.
  Cunningham's book of shadows: the path of an American traditionalist / Scott Cunningham. —1st ed.
      p.   cm.
  Includes bibliographical references.
  ISBN 978-0-7387-1914-6
  1. Witchcraft. 2. Wicca. 3. Magic. 4. Occultism. I. Title. II. Title: Book of shadows.
  BF1566.C835   2009
  133.4'3–dc22   2009025454

Llewellyn Publications
A Division of Llewellyn Worldwide, Ltd.
2143 Wooddale Drive, Dept. 978-0-7387-1914-6
Woodbury, Minnesota 55125-2989, U.S.A.
www.llewellyn.com

Printed in the United States of America

Contents

AMERICAN
TRADITIONALIST BOOK OF
SHADOWS

(original for printing)

The Blessing Prayer

In the name of Dryghtyn, the Ancient Providence,
which was from the beginning and is for eternity
male and female, the original source of all things:
all-knowing, all-pervading, all-powerful, changeless,
eternal; in the names of the Lady of the Moon
and our Lord the Horned One; in the names of the Spirits
of the Stones, rulers of the elemental realms:
Bless this place, and this time, and they who are
with us.*

(to be said before every rite, just after building the Circle of Stones)

* Scott Cunningham had a second version of this blessing prayer, in which he
  added deity names: "the Lady of the Moon, Diana, and our Lord the Horned
  One, Kernunnos."

HOW TO USE THIS BOOK

By Carl Llewellyn Weschcke

The book you hold in your hands is neither an ordinary book with its printed pages, nor a Traditionalist Book of Shadows.

Before I explain what the difference is and how to use this book, I want to tell you a few things relating to the author that may help your understanding.

The manuscript for this book had been "lost" among boxes of Scott Cunningham's writings since his death in 1993. His original proposed title was "American Traditionalist Book of Shadows." Due to events over the last quarter century, we felt that the word "Traditionalist" was no longer appropriate philosophically in association with the subject of Wicca.

Make no mistake, Scott Cunningham considered himself a Traditionalist in the original concept of that word: A *deep respect for tradition, especially for cultural or religious practice.* But our dictionary also offers an alternative definition: *The idea that all knowledge comes from divine revelation and is passed on by tradition.* It is this latter definition that gives us some difficulty.

Wicca is not "revealed knowledge" stemming from a single source that becomes established as theologically sacrosanct, but is instead a living tradition that is personally experienced and integrated into *your* life.

Wicca does not have a fixed theology administered and taught by a "Council of Elders" similar to historic authoritarian religions. There are a number of Wiccan churches established to administer to the needs of their membership for such purposes as marriage, funerals, personal counseling, etc., and there are many small covens bringing people together, but most practitioners of Wicca are "solitaries" who see themselves not separated from others by belief and lifestyle but fully integrated into the larger community while finding their spiritual strength from within.

It was mostly for these individuals that Scott wrote his books.

*   *   *

It's important to our understanding of how to use a Book of Shadows to clearly separate Scott Cunningham's writings from the anti-modernism and rigid fundamentalism characterized by that alternative definition of "Traditionalist." It is also important to understand that Cunningham's book is distinctly *American*, not Celtic or European.

Witchcraft is as old as the hills and is basically perceived as a system of nature-based magic and shamanism. Wicca is a modern nature-based religion that absorbed some practices and beliefs from traditional British Witchcraft. Yes, those beliefs and practices are mostly age-old, but they are also universal and readily adapted to the culture in which the practitioners are residents.

It is in this sense of attunement with the ebb and flow of the natural environment, and in the sacredness of those energies and the very soil of the locality, that Wicca has its experiential roots—and not in some claimed revelation from "on high" and held sacrosanct, to be explained to the rest of us by theological authorities.

Scott Cunningham was an American, initiated into a California coven at an early age because of his interests and devotion to natural magic. He had many teachers and he was a persistent researcher, but mostly he learned through practice, meditation, self-study, and experimentation.

Scott wrote more than fifty books on many aspects of Wicca and nature magic during his too-short life (June 27, 1956–March 28, 1993). He had tremendous respect both for his primary subject, Wicca, and for his readers. Yes, he had a deep respect for cultural and religious tradition, but not for historic or religious authority. His authority came from his own research and experience. He was very concerned that nothing he wrote could result in harm to his readers and never provided a ritual, a recipe, or a formula that was not thoroughly tested by himself.

*   *   *

All of this is important to the subject of this essay on *How to Use This Book*.

Traditionally, the student of Wicca interested in joining a coven was given that group's Book of Shadows to copy in longhand. In every sense, that handwritten book was the particular group's *sacred text*, containing basic rituals, celebrations and lore, the Laws, and the names and forms of the divine presence they integrated into their practices. These names and forms, the specific gods and goddesses, are among the most important secrets held by the group members.

But, once copied, the Book of Shadows also became the student's personal *grimoire*, a record book of his or her personal practices, meditations, realizations, experiments, and research. It is a *living* book, just like the life that Scott Cunningham lived.

And this is the point of my little essay. Respect your Book of Shadows, honor Scott and those who have gone before, but never become rigid in your beliefs or practices, for Wicca is a living religion, life is ever changing, and the entire meaning and purpose of your life is to grow and become more than you are. All of us are in the process of *becoming* a whole person, integrating body, emotion, mind, and spirit.

In our magical practices and celebrations we learn to inwardly tap into the collective wisdom (also called the collective unconscious) and bring into our personal consciousness the knowledge we need to grow.

In this book you will find the *Thirteen Goals of a Witch*:

    I.   Know yourself

   II.   Know the Craft

  III.   Learn

  IV.   Apply your learning

   V.   Achieve balance

  VI.   Resist temptations

 VII.   Keep your thoughts in good order

VIII.   Celebrate life

  IX.   Attune with the cycles of the universe

   X.   Breathe and eat correctly

XI.   Exercise both mind and body

XII.   Meditate

XIII.   Honor and worship Diana and Kernunnos

The only one of these goals that I believe needs a little explanation is the thirteenth. Diana and Kernunnos are indeed the names of a goddess and a god, and knowing their names and their form is the key to their worship, but they have also become abstractions and are not the universal aspects of divinity worshipped by all Wiccans. The gods and the goddesses have many names and many forms, and each group or each solitary practitioner must find their own. Deep inside you will find your god and your goddess, and you will know their names and forms.

*   *   *

This Book of Shadows is your book and your grimoire and can be adapted for group use or for solitary use. It is *your* sacred book.

How to use this book? Study *and* practice. If you are a solitary, begin by living in the cycles of the Sun and the Moon, i.e., by the seasonal celebrations (Sabbats) and the lunar phases of Full and New Moon (Esbats). Even alone, you can assume the roles of priest and priestess, and learn to experience the essence of those energies that are the *tides of life*. A time will come when you will know the presence of both the masculine and feminine forces we know as God and Goddess, whose divinity lives within our body, our feeling, our mind, and our spirit, and who live everywhere. You can speak to them inwardly and outwardly. You can see them in your heart and in your space. You can feel them and know them. And in your spirit you can be with them. If you prefer, you can perceive and receive their divine presence as singular rather than dual. We can't define the "Creator" in any way other than to know the divine is everywhere at all times, and is the Source of all that is.

Don't worry about doing everything exactly as it is in the book. See the book as a guide, not a rule book. You are the center of your universe, and your feet are planted in a particular place unique in space and time that will shape your experience. It is through this experience that you will grow and become more than you are—ever evolving—and become a whole person, able to handle the powers that will come to you through growth and development.

Crowley said that every man and woman is a star, and *so wilt thou be!*

*   *   *

Words from the Old Ones

The Book of Shadows is a Wiccan workbook containing invocations, ritual patterns, spells, runes, rules governing magic, and so on. Some Books of Shadows are passed from one Wiccan to another, usually upon initiation, but the vast majority of Books of Shadows today are composed by each individual Wiccan.

Don't believe the stories in most other Wiccan books that one single Book of Shadows has been handed down from antiquity, for each sect of Wicca seems to claim that their own is the original, and they're all different.

Although until recently a Book of Shadows was usually hand-written, today typed or even photocopied versions are quite common. Some Wiccans are even computerizing their books—to create, as friends of mine call it, the "Floppy Disc of Shadows."

To make your own Book of Shadows, begin with any blank book—these are available in most art stores and bookshops. If you cannot find a bound blank book, any lined exercise book will do. Simply write in this book any rituals, spells, invocations, and magical information that you have either composed or found elsewhere and would like to preserve.

Remember—all Books of Shadows are suggestions as to ritual, not holy writ. Never feel tied down to these words. In fact, many Witches use three-ring binders, shuffling around pages, adding or subtracting information from their Book of Shadows at will.

It is a good idea to copy your spells and rites by hand. Not only does this ensure that you've read the work completely, it also allows easier reading by candlelight. Ideally, all rites are memorized (there's nothing more distracting than having to read or glance at the book), or created spontaneously, but if you would read your rites, be sure your copies are legible by flickering firelight.

Excerpted from Wicca: A Guide for the Solitary Practitioner *by Scott Cunningham.*

Words from the Elder

O ye Daughters and Sons of the Earth, adore the Gods, and be blessed by them with the fullness of life.

Know that they have brought you to these writings, for herein lie the secrets of the Craft of Wicca, to serve and fulfill the keepers of the Wisdom, the tenders of the Sacred Flame of knowledge. Run the ancient rites with love and joy, and the Gods will confound those who work against you; but for those who work harm needlessly, their curse shall be the only fruit.

Remember, keep close to your heart, that you are of the Wise. No longer do you trod the ways of humanity; you skip on the path of Light, ever climbing from shadow to shadow to the highest realm of existence. But though we are bearers of truth, man does not wish to share our knowledge, so we meet in the shadows and run our rites beneath moon-filled skies. But we are happy.

Live life fully, for that is why we are here; refrain not from earthly life, for from such we grow and learn and understand, until such time that we are reborn to learn more, and to repeat this cycle till we have spiraled up the path to perfection, and can finally call the gods our kindred.

Walk the fields and forests; be refreshed by the cool winds and the touch of a nodding flower. The Sun and Moon sing in the ancient and wild places: the deserted seashore, the hushed valley, the raging waterfall. We are of the earth and should revere her, so walk lightly upon the ground and honor her.

Celebrate the rites on the appropriate days and seasons, and call the gods when the time is meet, but use the power only when necessary; not for frivolous ends. And know that using the power for harm be a perversion in the sight of the gods.

But for those who love and magnify love, as the dew-drop magnifies the sun, the richness of life shall be your reward, and all of nature will celebrate.

So love the gods, and harm none!

Blessed Be!

Before Time Was

Before time was, there was Dryghtyn; Dryghtyn was all, and all was Dryghtyn.

And the vast expanse known as the universe was Dryghtyn; all-knowing, all-pervading, all-powerful, changeless, eternal.

And space moved; Dryghtyn molded energy into twin forms, and so the gods were fashioned from Dryghtyn.

The God and Goddess stretched and gave thanks to Dryghtyn, but darkness surrounded them. They were alone, solitary, save for the Dryghtyn.

So they formed energy into gasses and gasses into planets and suns and moons; they sprinkled the universe with whirling globes and so the universe was given shape, by the hands of the God and Goddess.

Light arose and the sky was illuminated by a billion Suns, and the God and Goddess, satisfied by their works, rejoiced, and loved, and were one.

From their union there sprang the seeds of all life, and of the human race, so that we might achieve incarnation upon the Earth.

The Goddess chose the Moon as her living symbol, and the God the Sun as his living symbol, to remind the inhabitants of Earth of their fashioners.

All are born, live, and die beneath the Sun and Moon; and all things come to pass there under, as has been the way of existence before time was.

The Nature of Our Way

As often as possible, the rites should be held in forests, by the seashore, on deserted mountaintops or near quiet, tranquil lakes. If this is impossible, some chamber will suffice, if it is readied with fumes or flowers.

Seek out the wisdom in books, rare manuscripts, and cryptic poems, if you will, but seek it out also in simple stones and fragile herbs, and in the cry of the wild bird. Listen to the whisperings of the wind and the roar of the ocean if you would discover magic, for it is here that the old secrets are preserved.

Books contain words, trees energies, and wisdom books ne'er dreamed of.

Ever remember that the old ways are constantly revealing themselves; therefore be as the river willow, that bends and sways with the winds of time; that which remains changeless shall outlive its spirit; but that which evolves and grows will shine for centuries.

There can be no monopoly on wisdom; therefore share what you will with whom you will; but hide mystic ways from the eyes of those who would destroy, for to do otherwise increases their destruction.

Mock not the ways or spells of another, for who can say yours are greater in power or wisdom?

Take not one among you who serves to dominate you; who controls and manipulates your workings and reverences. Only within ourselves can true reverence for the old ones occur; therefore look with suspicion on those who would twist worship from you for their own gain.

All should share equally in the workings; thus none shall grow contemptuous of others in our way.

Honor all living things, for we are of the stag, and the salmon, and the bee; so destroy not life, save it be to preserve your own.

Blessings of the ancient ones on all.

The Law

1. This be the true and great law of the Wicca, ordained and consecrated for our use.

2. And this be the only law that the Wicca shall observe in council in the Circle.

3. All must obey the law if they be of the Craft.

4. The High Priestess shall be your mother, sister, and friend, and all shall obey her commands within the Circle, for she is the Goddess incarnate, and is to be respected. Common consent shall determine her successor, should she not appoint such by her own words.

5. The High Priest shall be your father, brother, and friend; and likewise you shall obey his desires within the Circle. For he is the God incarnate, and is to be respected. Common consent shall determine his successor, should the High Priest not appoint such by his own words.

6. The High Priestess and the High Priest shall each appoint aides, the Maiden and the Page, and their duties shall be to learn the High Priesthood such that they may perform all necessary rites and, with time, form their own coven. For the Craft must not die.

7. All shall be purified ere they step within the sacred Circle, which is anciently the Circle of Stones. All shall bathe and be purified with salt and herbs.

8. All shall be naked or robed, according to desire.

9. Give due worship to the Old Ones, as we have been taught.

10. All shall observe the Sabbats with due ceremony, and after the rites there shall be feasting and dancing, much merriment, to rejoice in the turning of the wheel of the year.

11. Likewise, all of the Wicca, once a month, shall meet to celebrate the March of the Moon and make magic in the God's names.

12. As often as possible, the rites shall be held in forests, by the seashore, on deserted mountaintops, or near quiet, tranquil lakes. But if this be impossible, then some chamber with adequate safety against discovery shall suffice, if it be properly purified with rosemary or frankincense.

13. As far as possible make all your actions honorable; for all that you do shall return to you three-fold: three times ill or three times good.

14. Seek out wisdom in books, rare manuscripts, and cryptic poems, if you will; but seek it out also in simple stones and fragile herbs and in the cry of the wild bird; listen to the whisperings of the wind and the roar of the ocean if you would master Wicca, for it be here that our secrets are preserved.

15. Books contain words; trees energies and wisdom that words ne'er dreamed of.

16. Make love with those who you will, but first be clean and free of bonds. And such shall not occur within the Circle, save it be for private rituals before the gods.

17. All shall be properly admitted before attending our Circles, or learning our secrets; thus shall our clan be kept from our oppressors who yet wrong us.

18. And because of such persecution, tell none who be not of the Wicca who your bond-sisters and bond-brothers be; nor tell them of the covenstead; nor the High Priestess; nor the High Priest. And speak not of your own membership: thus shall our persecutors be foiled.

19. Let each write and cherish his own book; and memorize what you can. When danger trembles on the horizon, destroy the book, or have a sister or brother secret it elsewhere, to save it from discovery. Rewrite the book as soon as danger is passed.

20. Let the tools be duly consecrated to our use, and put to no other.

21. None but the Wicca shall see our tools and rites, nor hear of them.

22. For even in these enlightened times, mankind eternally blames his own misery on the Wicca; he knows not that he brings it upon himself. Therefore we meet in the shadows, to preserve our love.

23. Teach those who come to you, if they be worthy. For to keep the Wicca alive it must spread, and to keep it from a worthy person be bane.

24. Those of the Wicca who break the law shall be given fair consideration in full coven.

25. By common consent, the punishment shall be agreed upon, which shall be light. For the second offense, too, a light punishment shall be agreed upon. But for the third offense of the same law, then banishment shall be handed down to the sister or brother, and she or he shall be utterly avoided.

26. But the punishment shall be light, save in case of grave danger or oath-breaking, for we be not as the new religion, with hellfire and angry jaws of death. We be of the old religion of wisdom and love, and communion with nature.

27. Any of the Wicca who knowingly brings enemies into our midst shall be banished and utterly avoided.

28. Honor all living things, for we are of the stag, and the salmon, and the bee; so destroy not life, save it be to preserve your own.

29. A law may be changed, by common consent, if it be out of sense for the day; but this is not to be done lightly, nor for convenience, but with love and wisdom and the good of the Craft in mind.

30. Blessings of the God and Goddess on all.

HERE ENDS THE LAW

Calling the God and Goddess

In some ways this is the heart of all Wiccan ritual, and indeed is the only necessary part. Wiccan rites are attunements with the powers that are the Goddess and God; all else is pageantry.*

The word "invocation" shouldn't be taken too literally. This usually refers to a spoken prayer or verse, but may also consist of music, dance, gestures, and song.

There are several invocations to the Goddess and God here. Feel free to use them when designing your own rituals, but remember that impromptu invocations are often more effective than the most ancient prayers.

If you do write up your own invocations, you may wish to incorporate a rhyme. Centuries of magical tradition attest to the value of rhyme. It certainly makes invocations that much easier to memorize.

Rhyme also contacts the unconscious or psychic mind. It drowses our societally, materially, and intellectually based minds and lets us slip into ritual consciousness.

When actually invoking, don't curse if you forget a word, mispronounce something, or entirely lose your train of thought. This is quite natural and is usually a manifestation of fatigue, stress, or a desire to be word perfect in the Circle.

Invocation requires a willingness to open yourself to the Goddess and God. It needn't be a pristine performance. As most rituals begin with invocation, this is, in a sense, the moment of truth. If the invocation isn't sincere, it won't contact the Goddess and God within, and the ritual that follows will be nothing more than form.

Practice invoking the Goddess and God, not only in ritual but daily, throughout your life. Remember: Wiccan practice isn't limited to Full Moons or Sabbats—it is a round-the-clock way of life.

In a more metaphysical sense, invocation is a dual-level act. It not only invokes the Goddess and God, it also awakens us (shifts our awareness) to that part of us that is divine—our inviolable, intransmutable essence: our link with the Old Ones.

---

* Though it should, of course, promote ritual consciousness. Outdoor rituals rarely need as much invocation because the Wiccans are already surrounded by natural manifestations of the deities.

In other words, when you invoke do so not only to higher forces but also to the deities that dwell within, to that spark of divine energy that exists inside all living creatures.

Excerpted from Wicca: A Guide for the Solitary Practitioner *by Scott Cunningham*

Calling the Gods

Arms outstretched:

> *Gracious Goddess, you who are the Queen of the Gods, the Lamp of Night; the Creator of all that is wild and free; the mother of woman and man; lover of the Horned God and protectress of all the Wicca; descend, we pray you, with your lunar shaft of power upon our Circle here.*

> *Horned One, you who are King of the Gods; Lord of the Sun; Master of all that is wild and free; father of woman and man; lover of the Moon Goddess and protector of all the Wicca; descend, we pray you, with your solar ray of power, upon our Circle here.*

Song of the Goddess

I am the Great Mother Binah, worshipped by men since creation and existing before their consciousness. I am the primal female force: boundless and eternal.

I am the Goddess of the Moon, chaste Diana, the Lady of all magic. The winds and moving leaves sing my name. I wear the crescent Moon upon my brow and my feet rest among the starry heavens. I am mysteries yet unsolved; a path newly set upon; I am a field yet untouched by the plow. Rejoice in me and be free.

I am the blessed mother Demeter, the gracious lady of the harvest. I am clothed with the deep, cool wonder of the earth and the gold of the fields, heavy with grain. By me the tides of the Earth are ruled, all things come to fruit according to my season. I am refuge and healing. I am the mother, giving life to the universe. I have been with you from the beginning and I am with you for eternity.

Worship me as Hecate, the unbroken cycle of death and rebirth. I am the wheel, the shadow of the Moon. I rule the tides of men and give release and renewal to weary souls. Though the darkness of death is my domain, the joy of birth is my gift. I know all things and have attained all wisdom.

I am the Goddess of the Moon, the Earth, the Seas. My names and strengths are many. All magic and power is mine, all peace and wisdom comes through me. I call unto thy soul; arise and come. I am that which is attained at the end of all desire.

I am Diana!

Call of the Great God

I am Kernunnos, the radiant King of the Heavens, flooding the Earth with warmth and encouraging the hidden seed of creation to burst forth into manifestation. I lift up my shining spear to light the lives of mankind and daily pour forth my gold upon the earth, putting to flight the powers of darkness and illuminating the minds of humanity.

I, too, am Herne, the Hunter, master of the beasts wild and free. I run with the swift stag's pace and soar as a sacred falcon against the shimmering sky. The ancient woods and wild places emanate my powers and the birds of the air bespeak my hallowedness.

I am also Keeper of the Key of Death and Rebirth; I guide the souls through the Gates of Death and beyond, to the lands of eternal Summer. For without death there cannot be birth, and without birth there cannot be life. Though my gift is death, my promise is life.

I am the Thousand-Named Sun of creation, the spirit of the stag in the wild, and the Lord of the Gates of Death. See in me the yearly cycle of festivals—my birth, death, and rebirth—and know that such is the destiny of all creation.

I am the spark of life, the Secret Seed, the giver of Peace and Rest, and I send my rays of blessings to warm the hearts and strengthen the minds of mankind.

Invocation of the Elements

Air, Fire, Water, Earth
Elements of Astral Birth;
I charge you now; Attend to me!

In the Circle, rightly cast,
Safe from psychic curse and blast;
I charge you now; Attend to me!

From cave and desert, sea and hill
By wand, blade, cup, and pentacle
I charge you now; Attend to me!
This is my will, so mote it be!

Dismissal of the Elements

Earth, Water, Fire, and Air
Elements both strong and fair,
Return to your abodes now; flee!
This is my will, so mote it be!

Creating Sacred Space

The Circle defines the ritual area, holds in personal power, shuts out distracting energies—in essence, it creates the proper atmosphere for the rites. Standing within a magic Circle, looking at the candles shining on the altar, smelling the incense, and chanting ancient names is a wonderfully evocative experience. When properly formed and visualized, the magic Circle performs its function of bringing us closer to the Goddess and God.

The Circle is constructed with personal power that is felt (and visualized) as streaming from the body, through the magic knife (athame) and, out into the air. When completed, the Circle is a sphere of energy that encompasses the entire working area. The word "circle" is a misnomer; a *sphere* of energy is actually created. The circle simply marks the ring where the sphere touches the earth (or floor) and continues on through it to form the other half.

Excerpted from Wicca: A Guide for the Solitary Practitioner *by Scott Cunningham*

The Places to Make the Circle of Stones

The best place to make the Circle is in a clearing in the woods, near a fast-running river, far from the places men go at night. There should be no thought that anyone will come upon you.

The crossroads was used in the past, where three roads meet, but this was dangerous as travelers still used roads at night, so there was danger that they would be discovered.

However, if you must work indoors, choose a room that is simple; large enough to contain the Circle, and unadorned if possible. Turn off all heating and cooling devices within the room, as well as all electrical appliances; they are unnecessary and may work against you. Unplug the phone too.

If your covenstead is indoors, try to have plants growing within, perhaps in the window or around the floor in the corners. These help give the room the necessary natural ambience. Never forget that Wicca is of nature.

Building the Circle of Stones

The Circle is built or "cast" before every Wiccan ceremony. To begin, ceremonially cleanse the area by sweeping with a broom. This should traditionally be done by a woman, if there are two or more meeting and one is a woman.

Next, set a large, flat stone to mark the quarters—one for each direction of the compass. Set the North Stone first. These stones represent the Spirits of the Stones, and are related to the Elemental forces. When these four stones are set, they should roughly mark out a square, with the distance between each stone roughly the same. This square represents the Earth plane on which we exist.

Now, take a cord and lay it out in a Circle, using the four stones as a guide. The stones should be outside of the cord circle. The Circle represents the Spiritual realms.

Circle size can be anything from four feet to twenty, depending on the number of celebrants and the size of the area you work in.

The preparations of the Circle are now completed. Set up the altar, with water in one bowl and salt in another. Light the candles and incense. Now proceed as follows:

Consecrate water by touching the surface of the water with the point of the athame, and saying:

I consecrate and cleanse this water
That it may be purified and fit to dwell
Within the sacred Circle of Stones.
In the names of the Mother Goddess
And the Father God,
I consecrate this water.
[Cunningham's other version of this Circle casting used
deity names: "*In the names of the Mother Goddess, Diana, and*
the Father God, Kernunnos ..."]

The salt is touched with the point of the athame, saying:

I bless this salt that it may be purified
And fit to dwell within the Sacred Circle of Stones.

In the names of the Mother Goddess
And the Father God, I bless this salt.

Stand facing North. Touch the point of the athame to the ground and trace the Circle, saying:

Here be the boundary of the Circle of Stones.
Naught but love shall enter in,
Naught but love shall emerge from within.
Charge this by your power, Dryghtyn!
[In an alternate version, Cunningham says: "*I charge you, O Circle, to be the boundary of the Circle of Stones, a guardian and protection to preserve and contain the power that we raise within you.*"]

Place the athame on the altar. Take up salt and sprinkle around the Circle, then carry the smoking censer around, then a candle, and finally sprinkle water. The Circle of Stones is now sealed.

Now, standing North, hold aloft the athame and say:

O Spirit of the North Stone,
Ancient One of the Earth,
We call you to attend our Circle.
Charge this by your power, Dryghtyn!
[In an alternate version, Cunningham says: "*O spirit of the North Stone, I do summon you to witness my rites and to guard the Circle against evil.*" This formula is repeated for the rest of the directions.]

Kiss the blade.

Face East, hold aloft athame and say:
O Spirit of the East Stone,
Ancient One of Air,
We call you to attend our Circle.
Charge this by your power, Dryghtyn!

Kiss the blade.

Turn to the South, hold aloft athame and say:
O Spirit of the South Stone,
Ancient One of Fire,

We call you to attend our Circle.
Charge this by your power, Dryghtyn!

Kiss the blade.

Turn to the West, hold aloft the athame and say:
O Spirit of the West Stone, Ancient One of Water,
We call you to attend our Circle.
Charge this by your power, Dryghtyn!

Place athame down on the altar. The Circle of Stones breathes around you. To strengthen, all join hands and circle clockwise, chanting or humming. Leader will stop when satisfied.

Rites may now begin.

Releasing the Circle of Stones

Facing North, hold aloft the athame and say:
Farewell, Spirit of the North Stone,
We give thanks for your
Presence here at our Circle of Stones.
Blessed Be!
[Cunningham's alternate phrasing is: " *O spirit of the North Stone, I*
give thanks for attending our Circle of love, and say hail and farewell, hail
and farewell."]

Kiss the blade.

Repeat to the East, South, and West, then return again to the North and hold aloft the blade.

The rite is ended; the Circle of Stones is no longer.

The Sabbats

In the past, when people lived with nature, the turning of the seasons and the monthly cycle of the Moon had a profound impact on religious ceremonies. Because the Moon was seen as a symbol of the Goddess, ceremonies of adoration and magic took place in its light. The coming of winter, the first stirrings of spring, the warm summer, and the advent of fall were also marked with rituals.

The Wiccans, heirs of the pre-Christian folk religions of Europe, still celebrate the Full Moon and observe the changing of the seasons. The Wiccan religious calendar contains thirteen Full Moon celebrations and eight Sabbats, or days of power.

Four of these days (or, more properly, nights) are determined by the solstices and equinoxes, the astronomical beginnings of the seasons. The other four ritual occasions are based on old folk festivals (and, to some extent, those of the ancient Middle East). The rituals give structure and order to the Wiccan year, and also remind us of the endless cycle that will continue long after we're gone.

Four of the sabbats—perhaps those that have been observed for the longest time—were probably associated with agriculture and the bearing cycles of animals. These are *Imbolc* (February 2), *Beltane* (April 30), *Lughnasadh* (August 1), and *Samhain* (October 31). These names are Celtic and are quite common among Wiccans, though many others exist.

When careful observation of the skies led to common knowledge of the astronomical year, the solstices and equinoxes (circa March 21, June 21, September 21, and December 21; the actual dates vary from year to year) were brought into this religious structure.*

Who first began worshipping and raising energy at these times? That question can't be answered. These sacred days and nights, however, are the origins of the twenty-one Wiccan ritual occasions.

Many of these survive today in both secular and religious forms. May Day celebrations, Halloween, Groundhog Day, and even Thanksgiving, to name some popular American holidays, are all connected

---

* Traces of this old custom are even found in Christianity. Easter, for example, is placed on the Sunday following the first Full Moon after the spring equinox, a rather "pagan" way to organize religious rites.

with ancient pagan worship. Heavily Christianized versions of the sabbats have also been preserved within the Catholic Church.

Some of the old pagan festivals, stripped of their once sacred qualities by the dominance of Christianity, have degenerated. Samhain seems to have been taken over by candy manufacturers in the United States, while Yule has been transformed from one of the most holy pagan days to a time of gross commercialism. Even the later echoes of a Christian savior's birth are hardly audible above the electronic hum of cash registers.

But the old magic remains on these days and nights, and the Wicca celebrate them. Rituals vary greatly, but all relate to the Goddess and God, and to our home, the earth. Most rites are held at night for practical purposes as well as to lend a sense of mystery. The Sabbats, being solar oriented, are more naturally celebrated at noon or at dawn, but this is rare today.

The Sabbats tell us one of the stories of the Goddess and God, of their relationship and the effects this has on the fruitfulness of the earth. There are many variations on these myths, but here's a fairly common one, woven into basic descriptions of the sabbats.

Excerpted from Wicca: A Guide for the Solitary Practitioner *by Scott Cunningham*

History of Yule

The Goddess gives birth to a son, the God, at Yule (circa December 21). This is in no way an adaptation of Christianity. The winter solstice has long been viewed as a time of divine births. Mithras was said to have been born at this time. The Christians simply adopted it for their use in 273 C.E. (Common Era).

Yule is a time of the greatest darkness and is the shortest day of the year. Earlier peoples noticed such phenomena and supplicated the forces of nature to lengthen the days and shorten the nights. Wiccans sometimes celebrate Yule just before dawn, then watch the sunrise as a fitting finale to their efforts.

Since the God is also the Sun, this marks the point of the year when the sun is reborn as well. Thus, the Wicca light fires or candles to welcome the Sun's returning light. The Goddess, slumbering through the winter of her labor, rests after her delivery.

Yule is the remnant of early rituals celebrated to hurry the end of winter and the bounty of spring, when food was once again readily available. To contemporary Wiccans, it is a reminder that the ultimate product of death is rebirth, a comforting thought in these days of unrest.

Excerpted from Wicca: A Guide for the Solitary Practitioner *by Scott Cunningham*

Yule Sabbat

The altar is set up, the candles and censer are lit, and the Circle of Stones is cast.

The cauldron is ringed with greenery: rosemary, pine, mistletoe, cedar, the evergreens representing the continuance of life amongst apparent desolation.

Each covener shall bring a dried twig or leaf and shall place these around the altar for use in the ritual.

The coven stands in a circle, holding hands, while the leader recites the Blessing Prayer.

The gods are invoked. Now the leader says:
Sorrow not, though the world is wrapped in sleep;
Sorrow not, though the wind doth blast;

Sorrow not, though the snow falls hard and deep;
Sorrow not; this shall soon be past.

The leader ignites the cauldron until it blazes freely.

All take up their twigs or leaves and stand near the cauldron. Each throws their offering into the cauldron, then all join into a circle around the altar, saying softly:

The Wheel Turns; the Power burns.

Repeat nine times.

Then the leader says:

Sorrow not, though the God lies slain by time;
For the Great Goddess is gracious; and she shall
bear him again.
Hail to the Queen of the Heavens!
Hail to the Queen of the Earth!
Hail to the Queen of the Oceans!
Hail to the Queen of Rebirth!

All repeat chant several times.

Then finished, the leader shall say:

Death is but the doorway to life.

Meditation, clairvoyant workings, and other works may be done.

The Simple Feast.

The Circle is released. Feasting and games follow.

One traditional practice is to decorate a Yule tree, although there is no actual ceremony for such things. The tree should be a living, potted tree, and should be planted or kept in the pot after the season has passed.

The Yule log is simply a representation of the death and rebirth of the God within the sacred fire of the Great Goddess. If so wished, the coven can select a proper log, carve or chalk the traditional figure of a man upon it, and set it alight in a fireplace or pit. This is unnecessary, however.

Yule

The cauldron should be in the South, wreathed with holly, ivy, and mistletoe. Light a fire within it. There should be none other light, save the altar candles, and those about the circle.

Cast the Circle of Stones.

Ring Dance while the High Priestess recites the incantation:

Queen of the Moon, Queen of the Sun,
Queen of the Heavens, Queen of the Stars,
Queen of the Waters, Queen of the Earth,
Bring to us the Child of Promise!

It is the Great Mother who gives birth to him,
It is the Lord of Life who is born again.
Darkness and tears are laid aside
When the Sun shall come up early.

Golden Sun of the Mountains,
Illumine the Land, Light up the World,
Illumine the Seas and the Rivers,
Sorrows be laid, Joy to the World!

Blessed be the Great Goddess,
Without beginning, without end,
Everlasting to eternity,
I.O. EVOHE, BLESSED BE.
I.O. EVOHE BLESSED BE.
I.O. EVOHE BLESSED BE!

Cakes and Wine.
The Circle is released.
Feasting and exchange of gifts.

History of Imbolc

Imbolc (February 2) marks the recovery of the Goddess after giving birth to the God. The lengthening periods of light awaken her. The God is a young, lusty boy, but his power is felt in the longer days. The warmth fertilizes the earth (the Goddess), causing seeds to germinate and sprout. And so the earliest beginnings of spring occur.

This is a Sabbat of purification after the shut-in life of winter, through the renewing power of the Sun. It is also a festival of light and of fertility, once marked in Europe with huge blazes, torches, and fire in every form. Fire here represents our own illumination and inspiration as much as light and warmth.

Imbolc is also known as Feast of Torches, Oimelc, Lupercalia, Feast of Pan, Snowdrop Festival, Feast of the Waxing Light, Brigid's Day, and probably by many other names. Some female Wiccans follow the old Scandinavian custom of wearing crowns of lit candles, but many more carry tapers during their invocations.

This is one of the traditional times for initiations into covens, and so self-dedication rituals can be performed or renewed at this time.

Excerpted from Wicca: A Guide for the Solitary Practitioner by Scott Cunningham

Imbolc Sabbat

The altar is set up, the candles and censer are lit, and the Circle of Stones is cast.

A symbol of the season, such as a crystal snowflake, a white flower, or perhaps some snow should be placed upon the altar. A candle for each covener present should be there also.

The coven stands in a circle, holding hands, while the leader recites the Blessing Prayer.

The gods are invoked. Now the leader says:

At Imbolc the land is wrapped in winter; the air is chilled and frost envelopes the tender green plants of the valley. The God of the forest and field

sleeps; and in that sleep he is born anew by the Great Goddess, as all must be;
And so what was sad is joyous; and what now sleeps or drowses
or falls lifeless shall spring up into existence and be reborn.
And therefore let us celebrate the coming of the God
and the labors of the Goddess!

All take a candle from the altar and light it from the Goddess' candle. The coven stands in a ring around the altar. The leader leads all in a slow walk around the Circle of Stones. When this has been traversed thrice, the leader calls a halt and places his or her candle in the cauldron, igniting it. The coven follows suit and all watch as the cauldron sparks and sputters with life.

The leader says:

Do you see the Light? That is the fire of Rebirth;
the fiery essence which is Life itself!

All sit and meditate upon the meaning of the ritual; of the cycle of reincarnation; of the meaning of death and, therefore, of birth itself.

When finished, if there is any divinatory work to be done, it is an excellent time for such.

The Simple Feast.

The Circle is released.

Feasting and games follow.

Imbolc

Build the Circle of Stones.

The High Priest should stand in the South, athame in his right hand, wand in his left, crossed on his chest. The High Priestess faces him, standing before him, and says:

Dread Lord of Life and Rebirth;
Lord of Life, Giver of Life,
You whose name is Mystery of Mysteries,
Encourage our hearts!
Let the light crystallize in our blood

Bringing us to rebirth.
For there is no part of us that is not of the Gods.
Descend, we pray you, upon your High Priest, _____.

High Priest then recites the Call of the Great God. High Priestess kisses him in acknowledgment. Cakes and Wine.

The Circle is released, and feasting takes place as usual.

History of Ostara

Ostara (circa March 21), the spring equinox, also known as spring, Rites of Spring, and Eostra's Day, marks the first day of true spring. The energies of nature subtly shift from the sluggishness of winter to the exuberant expansion of spring. The Goddess blankets the earth with fertility, bursting forth from her sleep, as the God stretches and grows to maturity. He walks the greening fields and delights in the abundance of nature.

On Ostara, the hours of day and night are equal. Light is overtaking darkness; the Goddess and God impel the wild creatures of the earth to reproduce.

This is a time of beginnings, of action, of planting spells for future gains, and of tending ritual gardens.

Excerpted from Wicca: A Guide for the Solitary Practitioner *by Scott Cunningham*

Ostara Sabbat

The altar is set up, the candles and censer are lit, and the Circle of Stones is cast.

Flowers decorate the Circle, the altar, and even the coveners themselves, if so desired. A potted plant, in bloom, should be placed upon the altar. The cauldron is filled with flowers and water.

The Blessing Prayer is recited.

The gods are invoked.

All gaze upon the plant while the leader says:

Now the Goddess frees herself from the icy prison of Winter;
Now is the Rebirth of Nature, when the land greens

nice again and the fragrance of flowers drifts upon the breeze.
This is the time of the beginning, when Life renews itself
and when the God of the Sun stretches and rises,
eager in his youth, but full of the promise of Summer.

The leader picks up the plant and holds it, concentrating on sending it energy. The plant is passed around the Circle, each covener striving to do the same. When all have sent the plant energy, it is replaced upon the altar. The coven decides where the plant should go: to a shut-in, a hospital, a friend, the wilds of the forest—wherever deemed most appropriate.

The leader next says:

As we love this plant; as we love all nature;
May we have within our hearts a love for all within nature;
thus is the Ancient Way of the Wicca, to love nature and all her creations.

Meditations may now be performed, if desired.

The Simple Feast.

The Circle is released.

Feasting and games follow.

A traditional game to play: gather an armful of flowers of various types, but only those that you can identify. Remember to pick them in the traditional way, explaining to the plant why you are taking the part and offering a token. Select common flowers, such as the rose, daisy, snapdragon—whatever is in season and plentiful.

Place all the flowers in a large vase. When the Circle is closed and the feasting has died down, bring out the vase and have all of the coveners come forth and take one flower. After this all explain why they chose their particular flower.

Afterward, the meaning and traditional magical uses of each plant are discussed, thus providing a clue to the natures of each person.

Other traditional activities include planting seeds, working on magical gardens, and so on.

Ostara (Spring Equinox)

Form the Circle of Stones.

The High Priestess lights a fire in the cauldron, saying at the same time:

> I kindle this fire today in the presence of the Mighty Ones,
> Without malice, without jealousy, without envy, without
> Fear of aught beneath the Sun, but the High Gods.
> We invoke you: O Light of Life: Be a bright flame before us,
> Be a Guiding Star above us, Be a smooth path beneath us;
> Kindle without our hearts a flame of love for your neighbors,
> To our foes, to our friends, to our kindred all,
> To all on this broad Earth, O Merciful Son of Diana,
> From the lowliest thing that lives
> To the name that is highest of all, Dryghtyn.

All leap the cauldron, if possible.

Cakes and Wine.

Release the Circle of Stones.

Feasting and games follow, if desired.

History of Beltane

Beltane (April 30) marks the emergence of the young God into manhood. Stirred by the energies at work in nature, he desires the Goddess. They fall in love, lie among the grasses and blossoms, and unite. The Goddess becomes pregnant of the God. The Wiccans celebrate the symbol of her fertility in ritual.

Beltane (also known as May Day) has long been marked with feasts and rituals. Maypoles, supremely phallic symbols, were the focal point of old English village rituals. Many people rose at dawn to gather flowers and green branches from the fields and gardens, using them to decorate the Maypole, their homes, and themselves.

The flowers and greenery symbolize the Goddess, and the Maypole the God. Beltane marks the return of vitality, of passion and hopes consummated.

Maypoles are sometimes used by Wiccans today during Beltane ritu-als, but the Cauldron is a more common focal point of ceremony. It rep-resents, of course, the Goddess—the essence of womanhood, the end of all desire, the equal but opposite of the Maypole, symbolic of the God.

Excerpted from Wicca: A Guide for the Solitary Practitioner *by Scott Cunningham*

Beltane Sabbat

The altar is set up, the candles and censer are lit, and the Circle of Stones is cast.

A small living tree shall be placed within the Circle near the altar.

Each covener present shall bring a small charm, token, or ornament they have fashioned to place on the tree.

A horn shall also be upon the altar, if possible. The Blessing Prayer is recited.

The Gods are invoked.

The leader says to the coven:

The God shines brightly in the sky;
the Goddess has brought forth a profusion of blooms
and leaves and living creatures upon the Earth.
Now the Goddess takes the God as her mate;
and all the land rejoices in a riotous blaze of color.
Let us present our gifts to the Divine Couple!

All place their tokens on the tree.

Now a young man, traditionally, takes up the horn and goes to the North point of the Circle of Stones. He blows once upon the horn and says:

Ancient God of the Summer, we welcome thee!

He turns to the East and repeats the ritual, then to the South and West.

Meditations and Clairvoyance.

The Simple Feast.

The Circle is released.

Feasting and games follow.

Beltane

Form the Circle of Stones.

Ring Dance.

If possible, ride poles. High Priestess leads with quick dance step, chanting:

O do not tell the Priest of our Art,

For he would call it sin,

For we will be in the woods all night

A' conjuring summer in.

And we bring you good news by word of mouth

For women, cattle, and corn,

For the Sun is coming up from the South

With Oak, and Ash, and Thorn.

Draw Down the Moon.

Cakes and Wine.

The Circle of Stones is released.

Dancing, feasting and games, if desired.

History of Midsummer

Midsummer, the summer solstice (circa June 21), also known as Litha, arrives when the powers of nature reach their highest point. The earth is awash in the fertility of the Goddess and God.

In the past, bonfires were leapt to encourage fertility, purification, health, and love. The fire once again represents the Sun, feted at this time of the longest daylight hours.

Midsummer is a classic time for magic of all kinds.

Excerpted from Wicca: A Guide for the Solitary Practitioner *by Scott Cunningham*

Midsummer Sabbat

The altar is set up, the candles and censer are lit, and the Circle of Stones is cast.

Each member shall, before coming to the rite, make up a petition of cloth filled with herbs such as lavender, St. John's wort, and vervain. This shall be tied with a red string. All shall place their petitions near the altar before the rite begins.

The coven stands in the Circle while the leader says the Blessing Prayer. *

The gods are invoked in the usual way. Now the leader says:

This is the time of the Balance.
This is the day when the hours of Light and Darkness
are evenly divided, when all of Nature is at a climax
and bursts forth with radiant energy.
The Goddess walks the fields, smiling at the crops,
while the God sends his rays to speed the harvest.
Now is the time of forgetting past cares and banes;
Now is the time for purification.

All take up their petitions as the leader lights the cauldron. As each throws his or her petition in the cauldron, they say:

I banish you in the name of Dryghtyn!

When all are finished, they return to form a ring around the altar, then move thrice around it.

The leader then says:

On this night of Summer's magic, when the God and
Goddess reign supreme; may we remember the balance
within us and within all nature; the changeless
balance that is the reflection of perfection.
Blessed Be!

The Simple Feast.
The Circle is released.

* *Editorial note: The blessing prayer here appears to be more suited to an autumn equinox/Mabon ritual. For another Midsummer ritual selection, see* Cunningham's Wicca: A Guide for the Solitary Practitioner.

Feasting and games follow, traditionally until dawn. Games of skill, contests, competitive sports, songs, and sacred plays are all traditional activities for this night.

Midsummer

Before the altar is placed the cauldron, filled with fresh water and wreathed with flowers.

Cast the Circle of Stones.

The coven stands around the Circle, the High Priest in the South and the High Priestess in the North. High Priestess holds the wand aloft, saying the following:

Great One of the heavens,
Power of the Sun,
We invoke you in your ancient names—
Michael, Balin, Arthur, Lugh, Herne—
Come again as of old into this your land.
Lift up your shining spear of light to protect us,
Put to flight the powers of darkness.
Give us fair woodlands and green fields,
blossoming orchards and ripening corn.
Bring us to stand on the Hill of Vision, and show
us the Lovely Realms of the Gods.

High Priestess hands the wand to the High Priest, who plunges it into the cauldron, then holds it upright, saying:

The Spear to Cauldron, the Lance to Grail, Spirit to Flesh, Man to Woman,
Sun to Earth.

He rejoins the coven.

The High Priestess takes up the sprinkler and stands by the cauldron, saying:

Dance about the Cauldron of Diana, the Goddess,
and be blessed by the touch of this consecrated water,
even as the Sun the Lord of Life, arises
in is strength in the sign of the Waters of Life.

The people dance deosil three times around the Altar and Cauldron, led by the High Priest, still bearing the wand. The High Priestess sprinkles each as they pass by her.

The Circle is released.
Cakes and Wine.
Games, dancing, feasting, as the High Priestess directs.
(The sprinkler: bind together fresh sprigs of any three herbs or wild plants, sacred to the gods or growing nearby. Knot nine times with white thread.)

History of Lughnasadh

Lughnasadh (August 1) is the time of the first harvest, when the plants of spring wither and drop their fruits or seeds for our use as well as to ensure future crops. Mystically, so too does the God lose his strength as the Sun rises farther in the south each day and the nights grow longer. The Goddess watches in sorrow and joy as she realizes that the God is dying, and yet lives on inside her as her child.

Lughnasadh, also known as August Eve, Feast of Bread, Harvest Home, and Lammas, wasn't always observed on this day. It originally coincided with the first reapings.

As summer passes, Wiccans remember its warmth and bounty in the food we eat. Every meal is an act of attunement with nature, and we are reminded that nothing in the universe is constant.

Excerpted from Wicca: A Guide for the Solitary Practitioner *by Scott Cunningham*

Lughnasadh Sabbat

The altar is set up, the candles and censer are lit, and the Circle of Stones is cast.

The altar is heaped with the first harvest; corn and fruit are traditional, as are sheafs of wheat. A figure of the God fashioned from bread is traditionally placed on the altar as well.

The leader recites the Blessing Prayer. The gods are invoked in the usual ways. Now the leader says:

This is the time of the First Harvest; when the
bounties of Nature give of themselves so that we may survive.
Such are the mysteries of Life; that all exists
so that others may; and that our quest for perfection
should not blind ourselves to others' quests;
The God gives of himself; but the Wicca do not sorrow;
for we give of ourselves that others may survive.
And the Goddess shines above us, and we rejoice.

The Simple Feast.
The Circle is released.
Feasting and games follow.
Corn dollie-making is a traditional game.

Lughnasadh

Form Circle of Stones.

High Priestess stands before the altar and says:

O Mighty Mother of us all, Mother all fruitfulness,
Give us Fruit and Grain, Flocks and Herds,
and children to the clan, that we be mighty.
By thy Rosey Love do descend upon your priestess.

All salute the High Priestess. Cakes and Wine.
The Circle is released.
Dancing, feasting.

History of Mabon

Mabon (circa September 21), the autumn equinox, is the completion of the harvest begun at Lughnasadh. Once again day and night are equal, poised as the God prepares to leave his physical body and begin the great adventure into the unseen, toward renewal and rebirth of the Goddess.

Nature declines, draws back its bounty, readying for winter and its time of rest. The Goddess nods in the weakening Sun, though fire burns within her womb. She feels the presence of the God, even as he wanes.

Excerpted from Wicca: A Guide for the Solitary Practitioner *by Scott Cunningham*

Mabon Sabbat

The altar is set up, the candles and censer are lit, and the Circle of Stones is cast.

The altar is decorated with acorns, oak sprigs, pine cones, cypress cones, ears of corn, wheat stalks, and other fruits.

Autumn leaves may be scattered around the Circle or on the altar. Chrysanthemums and marigolds are also traditionally upon the altar.

The coven stands in a circle while the leader recites the Blessing Prayer.

The Gods are invoked. The leader says:

The harvest is fully reaped; the God gives of himself
and journeys to the higher planes, and the sky grows dark.
Chilled winds blow in from the North as the
plants turn brown and wither.
But in the face of seeming extinction,
the Goddess sends forth her power, and by it we are sustained.
And thus in the dark days of Winter are we comforted
by the knowledge that all is a cycle; birth and death and rebirth.
Blessings upon the Great Goddess and Fallen God,
who journeys to the Lands of Summer!

The Simple Feast.
The Circle is released. Feasting and games follow.

Mabon (Autumn Equinox)

The altar should be decorated with symbols of autumn: pinecones, oak sprigs, acorns, or ears of grain.

Form Circle of Stones.

The coven stand about the Circle, the High Priestess invokes before the Altar:

Farewell, O Sun, Ever-returning Light,
The Hidden God, who ever yet remains,
Who now departs to the Land of Youth,
Through the Gates of Death,

to dwell in sleep
until the coming of Spring.
Yet even as he stands unseen about the Circle,
So dwells he within the Secret Seed,
The Seed of newly ripened grain,
The Seed of flesh hidden in the Earth,
The marvelous Seed of the Stars,
In him is Life, and Life is the Light of Humanity,
That which was never born, and never dies,
Therefore the Wicca weep not, but rejoice.

The High Priestess salutes the High Priest. Ring Dance three times around the Circle. Cakes and Wine.

The Circle is released.

Games and feasting. Dancing, if desired.

History of Samhain

At Samhain (October 31), the Wicca say farewell to the God. This is a temporary farewell. He isn't wrapped in eternal darkness, but readies to be reborn of the Goddess at Yule.

Samhain, also known as November Eve, Feast of the Dead, Feast of Apples, Hallows, and All Hallows, once marked the time of sacrifice. In some places this was the time when animals were slaughtered to ensure food throughout the depths of winter. The God, identified with the animals, fell as well to ensure our continuing existence.

Samhain is a time of reflection, of looking back over the last year, of coming to terms with the one phenomenon of life over which we have no control—death. The Wicca feel that on this night the separation between the physical and spiritual realities is thin. Wiccans remember their ancestors and all those who have gone before.

After Samhain, Wiccans celebrate Yule, and so the wheel of the year is complete.

Excerpted from Wicca: A Guide for the Solitary Practitioner *by Scott Cunningham*

Samhain Sabbat

The altar is set up, the candles and censer are lit, and the Circle of Stones is cast.

The leader says:

Tonight the great gates of the Lands of Summer open
for one we hold dear; the Sun God, his life waning,
has made the pleasant journey and enters into
the Land of Youth, until he comes forth again.
And this is the way for us all; therefore look
not upon death as a foe to be beaten, or as a friend to
be welcomed too early; simply see it as but another
step to your evolvement; an inevitable one,
as the rising of the Sun and the setting of the Moon;
no more, no less; thus can your life be lived fully,
without fear and worry.
For all are reborn by the Gracious Goddess,
and thus in the time of the greatest darkness there is the greatest light.

All meditate; communication with those who have passed on can be done if desired, but is not necessary.

The Simple Feast.

The Circle is released. Feasting and games follow.

Samhain

Walk or slow-dance with torches or candles to the covenstead. Cast the Circle of Stones.

High Priest leads High Priestess, and they both carry athames aloft, during the dance.

High Priestess invokes, after the dance:

Dread Lord of the Shadows,
God of Life and Giver of Life,
Yet is the knowledge of you,
the knowledge of Death.
Open wide, I pray you,

the Gates through which all must pass.
Let our dear ones who have gone before
Return this night to make merry with us
And when our time comes, as it must,
O Comforter, Consoler, the Giver of Peace and Rest,
we will enter into the Land of Youth
gladly and unafraid, as you yearly have done
so, long before our consciousness;
and when refreshed and rested among our dear ones,
we will be reborn again by the grace of the
Mother Goddess, Diana,
Let it be in the same place, and the same time as
our beloved ones, and may be meet, and know, and remember, and love them
again. Descend, we pray
you, upon your Priest _____.

Cakes and Wine.
The Circle is released.
Dancing and feasting. Divinations, as decided.

Full Moon Rites

The Sabbats are solar rituals, marking the points of the sun's yearly cycle, and are but half of the Wiccan ritual year. The Esbats are the Wiccan Full Moon celebrations. At this time we gather to worship She Who Is. Not that Wiccans omit the God at Esbats—both are usually revered on all ritual occasions.

There are twelve to thirteen Full Moons yearly, or one every twenty-eight days. The Moon is a symbol of the Goddess as well as a source of energy. Thus, after the religious aspects of the Esbats, Wiccans often practice magic, tapping into the larger amounts of energy that are thought to exist at these times.

Excerpted from Wicca: A Guide for the Solitary Practitioner *by Scott Cunningham*

Full Moon Rite

The Legend

Our Lady Diana would solve all mysteries, even the mystery of death, so when winter had come once again upon the earth and our Lord Kernunnos departed, the Goddess followed him. But the Guardian of the Portals challenged her: "Strip off your garments, lay aside your jewels; for naught may you bring with you into this land."

So Diana laid down her crescent crown, the moonstone and emerald bracelets from her ankles and wrists, the pearl earrings, the necklace of stars from her neck, the sacred girdle from about her body, and the veil of mist that covered her; she laid down all these things, and was bound, as are all who would enter the Realms of the Dead.

Such was her beauty that the God himself knelt and kissed her feet, saying; "Blessed be your feet that have brought you in these ways. Abide with me; let me place my cold hand on your heart."

She replied: "Why do you cause all things that I love and take delight in to fade and die?"

"Diana," Kernunnos replied, "it is age and fate, against which I am powerless. Age causes all things to wither; but when men die at the end of their time I give peace and rest, and strength so that they may return. But you, you are lovely; return not and abide with me."

And she did so for three days and nights; and the Moon grew dark and invisible. The God taught her the mysteries of death, and they loved and were one.

For there are three great mysteries of life: Love, Death, and Rebirth: and magic controls them all. For to fulfill love you must return again at the same time and place as the loved ones, and you must remember and love them again. But to be reborn you must die, and be ready for a new body. And to die you must be born; and without love you cannot be born, and these be all the magics.

Esbat

The High Priestess sweeps the covenstead with her broom to purify it. The altar is set up, the candles and censer are lit, and the Circle of Stones is cast.

The coven sits in a circle while the High Priest kneels before the High Priestess and says the following, with arms upraised:

Diana, you who are queen of the Gods,
the Lamp of Night, the Creator of all that is wild and free;
the mother of woman and man;
lover of the Horned God and protectress of
all the Wicca; descend, with your Lunar Shaft of Power,
upon your High Priestess, _____.

The High Priestess then recites the Song of the Goddess.

The High Priest rises and kisses the High Priestess in greeting. Magic is made.

The Circle is released.

Feasting and games follow.

Esbat

The leader sweeps the covenstead with the broom to purify it. The altar is set up, the candles and censer are lit, and the Circle of Stones is built.

The coven stands in the Circle while the leader recites the Blessing Prayer.

The gods are now invoked, using the evocations below or any others:

Ancient God of the Forest Deeps,
Master of beasts and Sun,
Here when the world is hushed and sleeps
Now that the day is done;
We call you in the ancient way
Here in our Circle round,
Knowing that you will hear us pray
And send your Sun-force down.

Lunar Goddess of the night
Who shines so far above
Who bathes the altar stone with light
And wisdom, joy and love;
We call you to attend our rite
And as we dance the round,
We pray that you will favor us
And send your Moon-love down.

A woman should invoke the Goddess, and a man the God.

If there is magic to be made, all gather and discuss, then the power is built up and sent forth by the dance.

If there is no magic to be made, all shall discuss the teachings.

The Simple Feast.

The Circle is released.

Feasting and games follow.

The Full Moon Rite

The High Priestess sweeps the covenstead with her broom to purify it. The altar is set up, the candles and censer are lit, and the Circle of Stones is cast.

The coven sits in the Circle, while the High Priest kneels before the High Priestess and says the following, with arms upraised:

Diana, you who are queen of the Gods, the Lamp of Night,
the Creator of all that is wild and free; the mother of woman and man;
lover of the Horned God and protectress of all the Wicca;
descend, with your Lunar Shaft of Power,
upon your High Priestess, _____.

The High Priestess then recites the Song of the Goddess. High Priest then speaks to the coven:

Tonight is the night of the Full of the Moon,
When her powers are at their peak, and when
mystic moonlight touches the shadows.
The Goddess' mystic jewel lights the heavens,
calling us to meet. Let us do her honor.

All sing the Moon Song:

Diana of the crescent barge, who travels in the Night,
Who lights the way to Sabbat ground with glowing Lunar Light;
We call you to be one with us, as one we call you nigh;
Charge us with your love and luck and bless us with your sigh.
For though we be but mortal flesh, who dance the ancient round,
We pray that you'll attend to us, and send your Moon-love down.

Magic is made.
The Simple Feast.
The Circle is released.
Feasting and games follow.

THE FULL-MOON RITE

The High Priestess sweeps the covenstead with her Broom to
purify it. The altar is set up, the candles and censer are
lit, and the Circle of Stones is cast.

The Coven sits in a circle while the High Priest kneels
before the High Priestess and says the following, with
arms upraised:

> Diana, you who are queen of the Gods,
> the Lamp of Night, the Creator of all that is
> wild and free; the mother of woman and man;
> lover of the Horned God and protectress of
> all the Wicca; descend, with your Lunar Shaft
> of Power, upon your HIgh Priestess, _____.

The High Priestessthen reciets the Song of the Goddess.

High Priest then speaks to the Coven:

> Tonight is the night of the Full of the Moon,
> When Her powers are at their peak and when
> mystic moonlight touches the shadows. The
> Goddess' mystic jewel lights theh heavens,
> calling us to meet. Let us do her honor.
> ásdfghjkjkjEjkjksjkgjkslkj

HkgkjRjkgkjksjkjkjkykjhjkhkjRojHdksjkjpkpkjhkrkjkpkjkskgkjhgkgHjkj

All sing the Moon Song:

> Diana of the crescent barge,
> Who travels in the Night,
> Who lights the way to Sabbat ground
> with glowing Lunar Light;
> We call you to be one with us
> As one we call you nigh;
> Charge us with your love and luck
> And bless us with your sigh.
> For though we be but mortal man flesh
> Who dance the ancient round,
> We pray that you'll attend to us
> And send your moon-love down.

Magic is made.
The Simple Feast.
The Circle is released.

ThgkSkjhjkjkjKgksjkjkjhjkjgjhgkjKojkjkys

Feasting and games follow.

The Full Moon Rite

The altar is set up, the candles and censer are lit, and the Circle of Stones is cast.

It is appropriate if some white flowers, crystal, or other Lunar symbols can be placed on the altar for this ritual.

The coven stands in a circle, holding hands, while the leader recites the Blessing Prayer.

The Gods are invoked in the usual way.

Now the leader says the following:

Tonight is the night of the Full of the Moon,

when her powers are at their peak and when mystic

Moonlight touches the shadows.

The Goddess' celestial jewel lights the heavens and the Earth,

calling us to meet. Let us do her honor!

All meditate for a few moments on the Moon.

Magic is made, after discussion and if necessary. This is also an excellent time for divination and magic-mirror workings.

The Simple Feast.

The Circle is released. Feasting and games follow.

Drawing Down the Moon

The High Priest kneels before the High Priestess, with arms upraised, and he says the following:

Diana, you who are the queen of the Gods,

the Lamp of Night, the Creator of all that is wild and free;

the mother of woman and man; lover of the Horned God

and protectress of all the Wicca; descend, with your

Lunar Shaft of Power, upon your High Priestess.

The High Priestess then recites the Song of the Goddess.

Cakes and Wine

High Priestess kneels, holding up the cup with both hands. The High
Priest lowers the tip of the athame into it, and he says:

By this I summon you, O Ancient Ones.

Bless this Wine and infuse it with your limitless love.

Let it become for your children the Life-force

that flows in all things; the manifested essence of the blessed elements.

In the names of Diana and Kernunnos, I bless this wine.

High Priest then kneels, holds up plate of cakes, on which the High
Priestess places the tip of her athame, standing, and says:

O Queen most secret and Lord most powerful,

Bless these cakes unto our bodies,

Bestowing health, wealth, strength, joy, and peace,

And that fulfillment of love which is perpetual happiness.

In the names of Diana and Kernunnos, I bless these cakes.

The High Priestess drinks and eats, then the High Priest and the rest of
the coven.

Consecrations

Many traditions utilize a specific ritual for the consecration of tools.
Some use the four elements (Earth, Air, Fire, and Water) in such rituals;
others, a sprinkling of blessed salt and consecrated water. Some type of
incantation should be created, borrowed, or adapted which aptly sums
up the ritual action. Such rites are usually quite short and rely far more
on the consecrator's energy than on the ritual form itself.

Excerpted from Living Wicca: A Further Guide for the Solitary Practitioner *by Scott*
Cunningham).

A General Consecration

To use with jewelry or various objects brought within the Circle of
Stones.

Place the object upon the pentacle, if possible. Say:

I conjure you, O _____, by the God and the Goddess,

by the virtue of the Heavens, of the Stars,

and of the Spirits of the Stones; by the virtue of hail, snow, and wind,
that you receive such virtue that you may obtain without deceit
the end which I desire in all things wherein I shall use you;
by the powers of the Mother Goddess, Diana,
and the Father God, Kernunnos, I consecrate you.

The tool should be censed, passed through flames, sprinkled, and then laid back on the pentacle, where it is sprinkled with salt.

Consecration of the Tools

Build the Circle of Stones. If possible, lay any tool touching an already consecrated one: athame to athame, wand to wand. Cast the Circle. Place the tool on the altar, touching it to the consecrated one, if possible, and say:

I consecrate you, O athame of steel (or pentacle of wood, etc.) ,
to cleanse and purify you so that you may serve
me within the Circle of Stones, that I might
perform the rites of Wicca. In the names of
the Mother Goddess and the Father God, you are consecrated.
[In an alternate version, Cunningham says: "*In the names of Diana*
and Kernunnos, you are consecrated."]

The tool is sprinkled with salt and passed over the censer, passed through flame, and then sprinkled with water, calling upon the Spirits of the Stones, the elemental forces, to consecrate it.

Then hold up the tool to the sky, saying:
I charge you by Dryghtyn; by the Powerful God and the Gentle Goddess;
by the virtues of the Sun, of the Moon, and of the Stars;
that I shall obtain the end that I desire while using you.
Charge this by your power, Dryghtyn!
[Cunningham's alternate version deletes this last line and instead finishes with: "*By the power of Diana and Kernunnos, be you consecrated.*"]

The tool should be immediately put to use.

Prayers, Chants, and Invocations

Chants are used to raise energy or to commune with the deities. Some of these invocations rhyme, and some do not. This simply speaks of my ability to compose rhyme, I suppose. But recall the power of rhyme—it links our conscious mind to the unconscious or psychic mind, thereby producing ritual consciousness.

Excerpted from Wicca: A Guide for the Solitary Practitioner *by Scott Cunningham (see note on copyright page regarding sources).*

Witches' Rune

Darksome night and shining Moon,
East, then South, then West, then North,
Hearken to the Witches' Rune,
Here I come to call thee forth.
Earth and Water, Air and Fire,
Wand and pentacle and sword,
Work ye unto my desire,
Hearken ye unto my word.
Cords and censer, sacred knife,
Powers of the Witches' blade,
Waken all ye unto life,
Come ye as the charm is made.
Queen of heaven, Queen of Earth,
Horned Hunter of the night,
Lend your power; give my spell birth
And work my will by magic rite.
By all the powers of land and sea,
By all the might of Moon and Sun:
As I do will, so mote it be,
Chant the spell and be it done:

Eko, Eko, Azarak,
Eko, Eko, Zomelak,
Eko, Eko, Diana,
Eko, Eko, Kernunnos! (times three)

Invocation to Diana

Diana! Diana! Diana!
Queen of all enchantresses
And of the dark night,
And of all nature,
Of the stars and of the Moon,
And of all fate and fortune!
Thou who rulest the tide,
Who shinest by night on the sea,
Casting light upon the waters;
Thou who art mistress of the ocean
In thy boat made like a crescent,
Crescent Moon-bark brightly gleaming,
Ever smiling high in heaven,
Sailing too on earth, reflected in the ocean,
on its water; Look down upon me
and guide me in my rites and in my life!

Preliminary Invocation

Lunar Diana,
Forestral Pan,
Be with us as woman
Worships with man.
Teach us the wisdom
Of living for life;
Help us create
Joy from strife.
Pan and Diana
Bless us this night;
Make us sacred
In your sight.

Preliminary Invocation

Diana of the crescent barge
Who travels in the night;
Who lights the way to Sabbat ground
with glowing lunar light;
We call you to be one with us, as one we call you nigh;
Charge us with your love and luck
And bless us with your sigh.
For though we be but mortal men
Who dance the ancient round,
We pray that you'll attend to us
And send your Moon-love down.

Full Moon Preliminary Invocation

Fair Diana, Goddess of the Rainbow,
of the Stars, and of the Moon;
the Queen most powerful of hunters and the night;
we ask of you your aid, that we may have the
best of fortune ever in our rites!

To Diana

Lovely Goddess of the bow!
Lovely Goddess of the arrows!
Of all the hounds and of all hunting
Thou who wakest in starry heaven
When the Sun is sunk in slumber;
Thou with Moon upon thy forehead,
Who the chase by night preferrest unto hunting in the daylight,
With thy nymphs unto the music of the horn—
Thyself the huntress, and most powerful;
I pray thee think, although but for an instant,
Upon we who pray unto you!

Isis Invocation

Isis of the Moon,
Thou who art all that ever was,
All that is,
And all that shall be:
Come, veiled Queen of Night!
Come as the scent of the sacred lotus, Charging our Circle
With love and magic.
Do thou descend upon our Circle
On this most magic of nights!

Healing Invocation to Isis

May Isis heal _____ as she healed Horus of all
the wounds which his brother Set, who slew his
father Osiris, had inflicted upon him. O Isis,
great magician, heal _____ , and deliver thou one from
all bad, evil, and typhonic things, and from every
kind of fatal sickness, and from diseases caused by
devils, and from impurity of every kind,
even as thou didst deliver thy son Horus.

Evocation of Hecate

O Night, faithful preserver of mysteries,
and ye bright stars, whose golden beams with
the Moon succeed the fires of day; the three-fold
Hecate, who knowest our undertakings and comest
to our aid when spells and arts we Wiccans use;
We ask that you be present as we perform this work
of retribution in your name.
Blessed Hecate, be with us here!

Prayer

Almighty Father of us all,
Lord of Death and Rebirth;
Lord of the Earth and the mountains,
Lord of the wild and free beasts;
Fill me with your Limitless Love!
Guide me in all that I do, think, and attempt
During this Circle. Blessed Be!

Call to Pan

O Great God Pan, return to earth again;
Come at my call, and show thyself to men.
Shepherd of goats, upon the wild hill's way,
Lead thy lost flock from darkness unto day.
Forgotten are the ways of sleep and night;
Men seek for them whose eyes have lost the light.
Open the door, the door that hath no key—
The door of dreams whereby men come to thee.
Shepherd of goats, oh answer unto me!

Invocation to Pan

O Great God, Pan, Father of man,
Shepherd of goats and Lord of the Land,
We call you to attend our rites
On this the magic night of nights.
God of the Wine, God of the Vine,
God of the Cattle and God of the kine;
Attend our Circle with your love
And send your blessings from above.
Help us to Heal; Help us to Feel;
Help us to bring forth love and weal.
Pan of the forests, Pan of the glade,
Be with us as our magic is made!

Evocation of Pan

O laughing God of the greenwood,
With your pipes and goat-like hooves,
Shepherd of creatures wild and free,
Join us here, and with your warmth
Let life be born anew!

Closing Chant

Merry meet,
And merry part,
And merry meet again!

Rites and Lore

Wicca possesses not one but several sets of rules. The most famous of these, which has been published in several different forms, originally stemmed from what is now known as Gardnerian Wicca.[1] Many other versions exist, and some covens create their own set of laws for use by their members. Underlying all such Wiccan rules is one basic concept: harm none.

Traditional Wiccan laws can be grouped into specific categories for study. Looking at these, and reading a few sample sets, should readily provide all that you need to write or adapt a set of laws for your tradition.

Excerpted from Living Wicca: A Further Guide for the Solitary Practitioner *by Scott Cunningham*

Curse

Whosoever releases the secrets of the Craft, such as are contained within this Book: May the Terrible Curse of the Goddess be upon your eyes: May the Terrible Curse of the Goddess be upon your ears: May the Terrible Curse of the Goddess be upon your mouth: May the Terrible Curse of the Goddess be upon your heart: May the Terrible Curse of the Goddess visit in the night the Oath-Breaker: For such Treachery sent millions of the Wicca to the Stake and Noose. You have taken the Oath: Mind the word of your Heart!

So Mote It Be!

---

1. For a fascinating look at the possible origins of these laws, see *Witchcraft for Tomorrow* by Doreen Valiente.

Thirteen Goals of a Witch

    I. Know yourself

    II. Know the Craft

    III. Learn

    IV. Apply your learning

    V. Achieve balance

    VI. Resist temptations

    VII. Keep your thoughts in good order

    VIII. Celebrate life

    IX. Attune with the cycles of the universe

    X. Breathe and eat correctly

    XI. Exercise both mind and body

    XII. Meditate

    XIII. Honor and worship Diana and Kernunnos

The Law of the Power

1. The Power shall not be used to bring harm, or to injure. But if the need arises, the Power shall be used to protect one's life, or the coven, or the Wicca.

2. The Power is to be used only as need dictates. It is acceptable to work for one's own gain, as long as it harms none.

3. Accept not gold for use of the Power, for it quickly controls the taker. Be not as the priests of the new religion.

4. Use not the Power for prideful gain, for such cheapens the great mysteries of Wicca.

5. Ever remember that the Power is the sacred gift of the gods, and should never be misused or abused. And this is the Law of the Power.

The Ways of the Power

1. Meditation or concentration. This in practice means forming a mental image of what is desired, and forcing yourself to see that it is fulfilled, with the fierce belief and knowledge that it can, and will, be fulfilled. This is called "Intent," and is all-important in magic.

2. Trance and projection of the Spirit, called "astral projection." Be careful with trances and astral projection. Used wisely, they can be of great benefit.

3. Rites, chants, spells, runes, charms, herbs. Of spells, the exact words matter little if the intent be clear, and you raise the true power and sufficiently thereof. Always in rhyme they are, there is something queer about rhyme. I have tried, and the same seem to lose their power if you miss the rhyme. Also, in rhyme the words seem to say themselves, You do not have to pause and think, what comes next? Doing this takes away much of your intent.

4. Incense, drugs, wines, whatever is used to release the Spirit. Be very careful of this. Incense is usually harmless, but sometimes it contains dangerous ingredients such as hemp. If you have any bad after-effects, reduce the amount used, or the time inhaled. Drugs are very dangerous if taken to excess, but it must be remembered that there are many drugs which are absolutely harmless, though people talk of them with bated breath. Be careful while taking mushroom (fly agaric). But hemp is especially dangerous, for it unlocks the inner eye swiftly and easily, so one is tempted to use it more and more. If it is used at all, it must be with the strictest precautions, and see that the person who uses it has control over the supply. Khat has nearly the same effect, but is difficult to obtain fresh. If any slightly dangerous drug is used, it should be doled out by some responsible person, and the supply strictly limited. [See publisher's note on copyright page for cautionary statement.]

5. The dance, and kindred practices. The ring dance within the Circle of Stones generates raw physical power and is an easy method

of raising energy. Private dances can also raise energy, but not so quickly; thus, concentration is better suited to solitary practice.

6. Breath control, bodily postures. Control of the breath is an excellent way to gain additional energy, especially when combined with concentration. The breath is slowly increased in speed until the power is released and sent off. The opposite mode, decreasing the breath, enables one to slip into meditation, deep relaxation, and astral projection.

7. Sex. The physical act generates enormous amounts of power, but it is difficult to control without intense concentration and much practice. If you desire more information on the magic of sex, ask your High Priestess or High Priest.

The most important aspect of magic making is the intent. You must know that you can and will succeed. This is essential in every operation.

You must also be safe from all interruptions, or from the mental fear of interruption, while making magic. If outdoors, find the remotest, most secluded glade; if indoors secure all entrances fastly.

And ever remember to look to the Moon, for constructive acts are performed during the waxing of the Moon, while destructive acts are best done during her wane.

Initiation

Much has been made, publicly and privately, of Wiccan initiations. Each Wiccan tradition uses its own initiation ceremonies, which may or may not be recognized by other Wiccans. On one point, however, most initiates agree: a person can be a Wiccan only if she or he has received such an initiation.

This brings up an interesting question: Who initiated the first Wiccan?

Most initiation ceremonies are nothing more than rites marking the acceptance of the person into a coven, and her or his dedication to the Goddess and God. Sometimes "power is passed" between the initiator and neophyte as well.

To a non-Wiccan, the initiation might seem to be a rite of conversion. This isn't the case. Wicca has no need for such rites. We don't condemn the deities with which we may have attuned before practicing Wicca, nor need we turn our backs on them.

The initiation ceremony (or ceremonies, since in many groups three successive rites are performed) is held to be of utmost importance to those Wiccan groups still practicing ritual secrecy. Surely anyone entering such a group should undergo an initiation, part of which consists of swearing never to reveal their secrets. This makes sense, and is a part of many coven initiations. But it isn't the essence of initiation.

Many people have told me that they desperately need to undergo Wiccan initiation. They seem to believe that one cannot practice Wicca without this stamp of approval. If you've read this far, you know that such isn't the case.

Wicca has been, up until the past decade or so, a closed religion, but no more. The inner components of Wicca are available to anyone who can read and understand the material. Wicca's only secrets are its individual ritual forms, spells, names of deities, and so on.

This needn't bother you. For every secret Wiccan ritual or Goddess name there are dozens (if not hundreds) of others published and readily available. At this moment, more Wiccan information has been released than ever before. While it once may have been a secret religion, today Wicca is a religion with few secrets.

Still, many cling to the idea of the necessity of initiation, probably thinking that with this magical act they'll be granted the *secrets of the universe* and *untold power*. To make things worse, some particularly narrow-minded Wiccans say that the Goddess and God won't listen to anyone who isn't an athame-carrying member of a coven. Many would-be Wiccans believe this.

It doesn't work this way.

True initiation isn't a rite performed by one human being upon another. Even if you accept the concept that the initiator is suffused with deity during initiation, it's still just a ritual.

Initiation is a process, gradual or instantaneous, of the individual's attunement with the Goddess and God. Many of the Wicca readily admit that the ritual initiation is the outer form only. True initiation will often occur weeks or months later, or prior to, the physical ritual.

Excerpted from Wicca: A Guide for the Solitary Practitioner *by Scott Cunningham*

Admission

Cast the Circle.

Draw down the Moon.

Ring Dance.

(Candidate is robed, blindfolded, and standing in the North, outside the Circle. High Priest[ess] takes up the athame and presses it against the candidate's breast.)

"You who stand in search of wisdom and love are poised between life and death. You who stand in search of wisdom and love must give the passwords to enter into the Circle of Stones which lies between the familiar realm of humanity and the unknowable reaches of the gods' domains. Have you two passwords?"

Candidate: "I have."

"Then, by your word, say them."

Candidate: "Love and Trust."

"By such words may you live your life, and with them enter into our Circle of Stones."

(Athame is taken away from the candidate's breast and placed on the altar. Candidate is kissed and led into the Circle.)

"Now is the Presentation."

(Candidate is led to the four directions, with the following invocation:)

"Spirit of the North Stone, _____ is properly prepared and shall be admitted into Wicca."

(Repeat for each direction, stating seeker's mundane name. Next, in the North of the Circle, say the following:)

"In ages past, when the Wicca were pursued by the Witch-finders and magistrates, and were in eternal danger, there was an ordeal which all who would be of the Wicca had to endure. This proved their loyalty, strength, and dedication to the Wicca, as well as their desire to enter into our clan. Today, in these happier times, this is no longer necessary, but ever be mindful that the persecution may flare up again without warning, at any time. Since you have entered into the Circle of Stones with Love and Trust, we shall accept this in token of your sincerity. Are you willing to swear your loyalty to Wicca, even though it should cost you your life?"

Candidate: "I am."

"And have you chosen a new name?"

Candidate: "I have."

"Then repeat after me as I say:" (High Priest[ess] says the oath, and the candidate follows it, phrase by phrase, and inserts his/her own Craft name:)

"I, _____ , who stand between the worlds, and within the sight of the gods, do of my own free will swear that I will keep fast and secure the secrets of the Wicca, except it be to a proper person, properly prepared, within a Circle such as I am now in. This I swear by my past lives, and by my lives to come, and may my weapons turn against me if I break this my solemn oath!"

(Remove blindfold after oath.)

The High priest[ess] takes up the bowl containing admission oil and describes a crescent on the candidate's forehead with the oil, saying:

"I bless you with the sign of the First Admission, Priest[ess] and Witch!"

(The candidate is now a Witch.)

Cords are removed. The High Priest[ess] places the Power hand on the crown of the new Witch's head and says:)

"I will all my power to you."

(New Witch is presented to the Four Portals:)

"Spirit of the North Stone, _____ is now a Priest[ess] and Witch. And ere you depart for your lovely realm, we say, hail and farewell, hail and farewell."

Cakes and Wine.

Dancing and feasting, and presentation of the admission gift(s).

Second Admission

Build the Circle of Stones.

(Witch stands robed and blindfolded outside the Circle. The High Priest[ess] comes before the Witch and says:)

"You who are a sister (brother) of Wicca have proved yourself to be worthy of admission to the second level. You stand near the Circle of Stones. The way is clear for you to enter, if you still desire. Do you seek to obtain the High Priesthood?"

Candidate: "I do."

"Then be admitted by my hand into the Circle of Stones."

(High Priest[ess] leads the Witch into the Circle, around the Four Portals, and finally before the altar. The High Priest[ess] holds up a mirror before the Witch, and removes the blindfold, saying:)

"Behold the God[dess]!"

(Candidate should see her/his own face in the glass.) "Such is the mystery of the Wicca."

(The mirror is placed to the East of the altar.)

"The High Priesthood is an awesome responsibility, requiring much faith and knowledge of Wicca. The secrets of Wicca will be at your fingertips; power and influence shall you have. In your coven you will be called upon to settle disputes, enlighten students, and initiate seekers. All this you must do with love and trust; love and trust must guide your life totally, and however much you may be tempted, never stray off the path of wisdom, for death touches those who do. Now, after these warnings, are you still desirous of attaining the High Priesthood?"

Candidate: "I am."

"Then swear the oath."

(High Priest[ess] says the oath, and the Witch repeats phrase by phrase:)

"I, _____, do swear that I shall act as a true vehicle of the Goddess; that I shall nurture the growth of both Wicca and the souls that come to me; that I shall rule my coven with love and trust, and that I shall never betray any of the Wicca to those who are not, nor shall I betray the trust that my High Priest[ess] has in me. This I swear by my past lives and hopes of future lives to come, and may the forces turn against me should I break this my oath."

(High Priest[ess] takes up the bowl of admission oil and anoints the forehead of the Witch with a pentagram, saying:)

"I bless you with the sign of the Second Level, High Priest[ess]."

(The candidate is now a High Priest[ess]. A kiss is given in celebration. The Circle of Stones is released.

Cakes and Wine, feasting, and merriment follow.

Third Level Admission: The Covening

(The High Priestess and High Priest form the Circle of Stones together, working in harmony, in token of their future Craft life together. When finished, they will stand before the altar, the High Priestess to the left, and invoke the gods thusly:)

"In the name of Dryghtyn, the ancient providence, which was from the beginning, and is for eternity male and female, the original source of all things: all-knowing, all-pervading, all-powerful, changeless, eternal. In the name of the Lady of the Moon, Diana, and the Lord of the Sun, Kernunnos: bless our covening that it may spread the growth and ensure the survival of Wicca. Aid in building our coven into a gathering of love and trust, that it may be fit in your sight. Blessed Be, Great Ones, Blessed Be!"

The High Priestess and High Priest kiss. The High Priestess traces the sign of the Third Level on the High Priest's forehead, and then the High Priest does so on the High Priestess' forehead, with admission oil.

The High Priestess then holds her athame over the altar. The High Priest touches the tip of his athame under the High Priestess' and they stand thus, visualizing their forces and energies mingling together.

They then exchange athames and hold them to their hearts for thirteen heartbeats, then give them back.

They say:

"Thus is the new coven of _____ and _____ begun.

It shall be known as the coven of _____ and shall hereafter

be known as the Coven of _____ on all planes and spaces. Diana and Kernunnos, in love and trust, is this coven so established."

The High Priestess and High Priest now sit and discuss all matters pertaining to their future coven. When all has been settled to both of their minds, they will cut the Circle and the rite will be ended.

Handfasting

The covenstead is decorated with flowers and fruit. More flowers and a floral crown are on the altar, which is itself decorated with flowers.

Build the Circle of Stones.

The couple, robed splendidly, kneel, the woman on the left. The High Priest invokes:

O Mother of love,
Who has been called Venus, Ishtar, Habondia.
Aphrodite, Isis, Cerridwen: Extend your hand of
protection to this daughter and son of man.
Deflect evil from them, and confound those who
would blaspheme against the true light of your wisdom.

The couple stand, and they are anointed to their level on the forehead with handfasting oil.

The couple kneels again and the High Priest addresses them:

Know that it is the decree of fate that you are to be united,
so long as love shall last. In vain against the stars preach the monk
and priest; what shall be, shall be.
Wherefore take hope and joy, O children of time.
And now, as I join your hands, I betroth your souls.

The High Priest consecrates the crown with Earth, Air, Fire, and Water and passes it over the head of the man and then over the head of the woman, placing it there.

High Priest holds his left hand over the couple, raises his right, and says:

May Dryghtyn, the Spirits of the Stones, and the powerful God, Kernunnos,
and the gentle Goddess Diana, attest the betrothal of these young hearts.
O Circle of Stones and altar of power, attest the betrothal
of these young hearts.
O Sun and Moon, attest the betrothal of these young hearts.
While the forms are divided, may the souls cling together,
Sorrow with sorrow, joy with joy,
And when at length bride and bridegroom are one,
O Stars, may the trouble with which you are charged
have exhausted its burden; may no danger molest,
and no malice disturb; but over the marriage bed, shine in peace, O Stars.

Now the couple swear; each in turn:

In the Sight of Dryghtyn, the Ancient Providence,
and Diana and Kernunnos,
between the familiar realm of humanity
and the unknown reaches of the God's domains,
and surrounded by the Spirits of the Stones,
I take you to my hand at the setting of the Sun,
the rising of the Stars.

The couple now jump the broomstick. They kneel as the High Priestess sweeps away all evil influences behind them and out of the Circle toward the south.

Release the Circle.

Cakes and Wine.

Dancing, feasting, much, merriment.

NOTE: The actual handfasting may be done by either the High Priestess or the High Priest. Foods traditionally include those of the dairy and fruits and flowers.

Recipes for the Feast

Food is magic. Its power over us is undeniable. From the sweet, rich lure of a freshly baked brownie to an exquisitely steamed artichoke, food continues to seduce us.

Food is life. We can't continue to live without its magic. Food, however, also harbors energies. When we eat, our bodies absorb those energies, just as they absorb vitamins, minerals, amino acids, carbohydrates, and other nutrients. Though we may not be aware of any effect other than a sated appetite, the food has subtly changed us.

In times of scarcity as well as plenty, people around the world have subjected food to religious reverence. Rice in Asia; fruit throughout Europe; grains in Africa; pomegranates and beer in the Near East; acorns and pine nuts in the American Southwest; bananas and coconuts in the Pacific; vegetables in tropical America—these foods have all played significant roles in religious and magical rituals.

Sacred meals are shared with the goddesses and gods (or their priestesses and priests). Today, eating with others is still an act of energy sharing, bonding, and trust.

The magic of the hunt and the sacredness of gathering rituals in fields and groves are still remembered by a few isolated peoples. Most of us now, however, buy presliced bread, gather our fruits and vegetables from gleaming counters, and hunt in refrigerated cases.

As we've lost the knowledge of the old magics, so too have we forgotten the mystic lore of food. But timeless energies still vibrate within our meals. They wait for us to sense and use them. Lengthy magical spells aren't required, though a simple ritual is necessary to boost the food's effectiveness.

Eating is a merging with the earth. It is a life-affirming act. Ritually preparing and eating specific foods is an effective method of enhancing and improving our lives.

Excerpted from Cunningham's Encyclopedia of Wicca in the Kitchen *by Scott Cunningham*

Winter Sabbat Wine

1 large or 3 small bottles red wine

3 oranges

3 tablespoons whole cloves

Ground nutmeg

3 cinnamon sticks

1 cup brandy

1 cup apple cider

Pour wine into non-metallic, heat-proof container. Wash oranges well. Cut two into thin slices and add to the wine. Stud the remaining orange with cloves, marking out good-fortune runes, and add to the wine. Dust the top of the wine with ground nutmeg and then add remaining ingredients. Warm slowly, but do not boil. Serve on windy nights after the Winter Sabbats.

Summer Sabbat Wine

1 large or 3 small bottles white wine

Fruits in season (melon, citrus, berries, cherries, pineapple, apricots, pears, cherries, etc.)

Rose petals, fresh

1 lemon

1 cup grapefruit juice

Pour wine into container. Chop fruit (about one cup or so, according to taste and availability) and add to wine. Let sit overnight. Before the ritual cut up the lemon into slices, brush with freshly milled coconut (optional) and add to wine. Pour in grapefruit juice and finally float the rose petals on top. Serve well chilled.

Beltane Wine

3 bottles chilled dry white wine

Handful fresh woodruff

1 pint strawberries

Pour wine into non-metallic bowl. Shred the woodruff through your hands and add to the wine. Cover with cloth and let steep overnight in a cool place.

In the morning, strain through cheesecloth and return to bowl. Directly before the ritual add sliced strawberries. Chill and remove just before the feast so that it will be cold.

BELTANE WINE

3 bottles chilled dry white wine
handful fresh woodruff
1 pint woodruff strawberries

Pour wine into non-metallic bowl. Shred the woodruff through your hands and add to the wine. Cover with cloth and let steep overnight in a cool place.
In the morning, strain through cheesecloth and return to bowl. Directly before the ritual add sliced strawberries. Chill and remove just before the feast so that it will be cold.

Samhain Warmer

1 pumpkin
Apple cider
Cranberry juice
Ginger ale
Rum
Raisins

Slice off top of pumpkin, scoop out seeds and set these aside. Pour equal parts of the liquids to fill the pumpkin; remove and warm until nearly boiling just before feast. Pour back into pumpkin, add a handful of raisins, and set out for coveners to enjoy.

Wash, then dry seeds and toast lightly in the oven, then eat with salt!

Mulled Cider

2 quarts apple cider
7 cinnamon sticks
1 whole orange
Cloves
Nutmeg
1 cup mead (optional)

Warm cider in non-metallic pan until hot; add cinnamon sticks. Let set on low heat, steeping. Meanwhile, stud orange with cloves. Add to cider, then dust with about 1 teaspoon nutmeg. Mead can be added if desired. Serve while warm, but not quite hot. Perfect for all fall and winter Sabbats.

Soft Mead

For a small amount of non-alcoholic mead, take one quart spring water, one cup honey, one lemon cut into slices, one-half teaspoon nutmeg. Boil in non-metallic pot, removing the scum as it rises with wooden spoon. Add pinch of salt, and juice of one-half lemon. Strain and cool. Drink in place of alcoholic mead, wine, etc.

Substitutes

Other good liquids to serve in place of wine within the Circle include:

Sabbats: apple juice, grape juice, grapefruit juice, orange juice, pine-apple juice, oriental tea

Full Moon celebrations: lemonade, apricot juice, peppermint tea, mango nectar, milk

Any good herbal teas may also be used. Hard (alcoholic) drinks should be used with discretion, for the meal is in the presence of the Gods!

Crescent (or Moon) Cakes

(Full Moon celebrations, Sabbats)

    1 cup almonds, finely grated
    1¼ cups flour
    ¼ cup confectioner's sugar
    ½ cup butter
    1 egg yolk

Combine almonds, flour, and sugar. Work in butter and egg yolk with hands until well blended. Chill. Pinch off pieces of dough the size of walnuts, shape into crescents. Place on greased sheets and bake at 325°F for about 20 minutes.

Sabbat Cakes

(Serve on Sabbats)

    3 teaspoons honey
    ⅓ cup shortening
    ½ cup brown sugar
    ¼ cup apple sauce
    1 tablespoon white wine

1½ cups whole grain flour
1½ cups oatmeal
¼ teaspoon baking soda
½ teaspoon salt
½ teaspoon allspice

Blend together honey, shortening, sugar, applesauce, and wine. Add remaining ingredients, mix well. Form into a ball of dough. Roll out ¼ inch thick and cut with a crescent-shaped cutter. Place on greased cookie sheets and bake at 350° for 15 minutes or until golden brown.

Cyder Cake

(Samhain, Yule)
3 cups sifted flour
½ teaspoon baking soda
½ teaspoon grated nutmeg
½ cup softened butter
1½ cups sugar
2 eggs, well beaten
½ cup cyder (cider)
Oven: 350°F

In a mixing bowl, sift together flour, baking soda, and nutmeg. Set aside.

In another, larger mixing bowl, beat together well the butter and sugar. Add eggs and beat well. Then add flour mixture and cider alternately, beginning and ending with the flour.

Spoon batter into a well-buttered 9¼ x 5½ x 2¾ loaf pan, and bake for 1 hour in preheated oven, or until a toothpick inserted into the center of the cake comes out dry.

Cardamom Apple Pie

(Samhain, Yule)

Unbaked pastry for 9-inch 2-crust pie

5 cups sliced tart apples

¾ cup brown sugar (substitute slightly less than 1 cup honey)

2 tablespoons butter

1 teaspoon ground cardamom seed

¾ teaspoon pure vanilla extract

Line 9-inch pie plate with half of pastry; arrange apple slices on pastry, sprinkling with brown sugar or honey between layers. Dot with butter. Add cardamom and vanilla. Roll remaining pastry in circle; place pastry circle over apples; seal and flute edges. Make slits into top of pastry (sign of Venus ♀).

Bake in preheated hot oven (400°F) 10 minutes; reduce oven temperature to 350 and continue baking for 30 to 35 minutes, or until crust is lightly browned.

CARDAMOM APPLE PIE

(Samhain, Yule)

Unbaked pastry for 9-inch 2-crush pie
5 cups sliced tart apples
1/4 cup brown sugar (substitute slightly less than ¼ cup hoi
2 tablespoons butter
1 teaspoon ground cardamom seed
3/4 teaspoon pure vanilla extract

Line 9-inch pie plate with half of pastry; arrange apple-slices in pastry, sprinkling with brown sugar or honey between laywers. Dot with butter. Add cardamom and vanilla. Roll remaining pastry in circle; place pastry circle over apples; seal and flute edges. Make slits into top of pastry: (sign of Venus)

Bake in preheated hot oven (400°F.) 10 minutes; reduce oven temperature to 350 and continue baking for 30 to 35 minutes or until crust is lightly browned.

Marigold Custard

1 pint milk

1 cup marigold petals

1 teaspoon salt

3 tablespoons sugar

Small piece vanilla bean

3 egg yolks

⅛ teaspoon nutmeg

⅛ teaspoon allspice

½ teaspoon rose water

Pound marigold petals in a mortar, or crush them with a spoon, and scald with the milk and vanilla bean. Remove the vanilla bean, and add slightly beaten yolks of eggs, salt, and sugar mixed with the spice. Cook until the mixture coats the spoon. Add rosewater and cool. This makes a good sauce for a blancmange. It may be poured into a dish without cooking, and then baked like custard. Serve with beaten cream, add orange water, and garnish with marigold blossoms.

MARIGOLD CUSTARD

1 pint milk
1 cup marigold petals
¼ teaspoon salt
3 tablespoons sugar
  small piece vanilla bean
3 egg yolks
1/8 teaspoon nutmeg
1/8 teaspoon allspice
½ teaspoon rose water

Pound marigold petals in a mortar, or crush them with a spoon, and scald with the milk and vanilla bean. Remove the vanilla bean, and add slightly beaten yolks of eggs, salt and sugar mixed with the spice. Cook until the mixture coats the spoon. Add rosewater and cool. This makes a good sauce for a blanc mange. It may be poured into a dish without cooking, and then baked like custard. Serve with beaten cream, and garnish with marigold blossoms.
add orange water

Colcannon

(Samhain)

    4 large or 6 medium potatoes

    Cold water

    1 teaspoon salt

    4 cups finely shredded cabbage

    2 cups boiling salted water

    1 cup warm milk

    Salt and pepper

    4 tablespoons butter, melted

Peel potatoes, remove eyes. Cut large potatoes in quarters, or medium potatoes in half. Place in large saucepan, cover with cold water. Add salt, bring to boil. Reduce heat to low; cook approximately 20 minutes or until fork-tender. Drain well, return to saucepan. Place tea towel between pan and lid; steam over very low heat 10 minutes.

    Meanwhile, cook cabbage in boiling salted water 5 minutes. Drain well, reserve.

    Mash potatoes with warm milk. Season with salt and pepper. Beat in cooked cabbage to form pale-green fluff. Place in warm serving dish. Make well in center, pour in melted butter. Serve immediately. Serves half a coven.

Rowan Jelly

To make about four pounds:

    2 pounds rowans

    1 pound crab apples

    2 pints water (5 cups)

    Granulated sugar

Wash the berries, remove any damaged ones, and snip off the excess stalks. Put the fruit into a pan with the apples, roughly chopped. Add the water, then simmer the fruits until soft—about 30 minutes. Strain the liquid through a scalded jelly bag and leave it overnight to drip—do not be tempted to squeeze the bag or a cloudy jelly will result.

Next day measure the liquid and add 1 lb. sugar to every pint of juice (2 cups to 22 cups liquid). Gradually dissolve the sugar in the syrup, then bring the jelly to a boil and boil it until setting point—about 15 minutes. Test for set by placing a spoonful on a plate, letting it cool and then pushing the surface with your finger. If it wrinkles, the jam is ready. Put into warm, clean jars, seal covers, label, and store until required. May be used all year round, especially served with thick soups and stews and meat during the dark months of the year (Samhain to Beltane).

Samhain Cake

Baked into this cake are several charms representative of the gods and good fortune. These should be wrapped in aluminum foil or waxed paper before being added to the cake batter, and can be made of any (nonpoisonous) substance desired.

1 cup butter
1 cup sugar
4 medium eggs
3 cups self-rising flour
Grated rind of an orange
3 tablespoons milk
8-inch cake tin, greased, and base lined with waxed paper

Beat butter until soft, add sugar and cream, beating together to a soft and fluffy texture. Beat in the eggs one at a time, adding a little sifted flour if the mixture begins to curdle. Stir in the charms, carefully wrapped, the orange rind with the milk, and all the flour to make a soft dropping consistency. Turn the mixture into the pan and spread it to the sides, leaving the center slightly hollow.

Bake at 350°F for 1 to 1¼ hours or until the cake is well risen, golden brown, and slightly shrinking away from the sides of the tin. Leave the cake to cool.

Icing

⅜ cup (6 tablespoons) apricot jam (or orange
marmalade)
3¾ cups confectioner's sugar
Juice of 1 orange
A little orange coloring

Split the cake in half, spread it with the jam, then sandwich the pieces
back together again and stand the cake on a wire tray. Mix the orange
juice with the icing sugar, adding warm water if necessary, to make an
icing that thickly coats the back of a spoon. Color the icing orange, then
pour it over the cake, guiding it to the edges and letting it flow over the
sides. Leave the cake to dry, then decorate.

Saffron Rice

A Sabbat food served with sweet potato casserole, broccoli with caper
sauce, hot cornbread, flaming apples and fruits in season, and, of course,
baked ham in cider (Yule).

1½ tablespoons butter
1½ teaspoons saffron (Spanish strand type)*
2 teaspoons crystal (rock) salt
1½ cups rice, about 3/4 lb.**
1½ tablespoons vermouth

Heat vermouth to blood temperature, add saffron, stir. In a heavy saucepan heat rice, water and salt. When it starts to boil, add the butter to
keep from frothing and boiling over. As it boils, add the vermouth mixture. Stir, then cover and simmer over slow heat for fifteen minutes, or
until rice has absorbed all the water.

*1 teaspoon saffron to one cup rice. To get the best coloring power, it
should first be steeped in a warm, not hot, alcoholic bath.

**Note: this recipe is fragmented. For instance, it doesn't record how
much water to use for the rice. Follow directions on package for this, as
it depends on the type of rice being used.

Saffron Cake*

(Yule, Candlemas)

½ ounce yeast

8 tablespoons flour

4 ounces butter

2 ounces sugar

1 tablespoon chopped candied peel

1 egg

½ teaspoon mixed spice (opt.)

1 gill (¼ cup) warm water

Pinch salt

4 teaspoons powdered saffron

3 tablespoons seedless raisins

Dissolve the yeast in the tepid water and mix in about 2 tablespoons of flour. Mix well, cover with a cloth, and leave for about one hour or until twice the size. Sift the rest of the flour into a basin with the salt and spice, if you are using it. Cream butter and sugar, add the beaten egg and the saffron, mixed well with a teaspoon of water. Combine with the flour and add to the yeast dough. Knead well, adding raisins and peel, put into a greased loaf tin, and leave to rise again for about 2 hours. Cook in moderate oven for 1½ hours.

*This cake can be made without yeast, using a teaspoon of baking powder and 2 eggs for the same ingredients listed. It can be made into small buns for coven purposes. If baking powder is used, it should not be left to rise.

The Simple Feast

Hold up cup of wine between the hands to the sky, and say:

Gracious Goddess of Abundance,
Bless this wine and infuse it
with your limitless love.
in the names of the Mother Goddess
and the Father God,
I bless this wine.

Hold up plate of cakes with both hands to the sky, and say:

Powerful God of the Harvest,
Bless these cakes and infuse
them with your limitless love.
In the names of the Mother Goddess
and the Father God,
I bless these cakes.

All eat, and drink, sitting in the Circle.

An Herbal Grimoire

In centuries past, when the nightmares we know of as cities had yet to be born, we lived in harmony with the earth and used her treasures wisely. Many knew the old magics of herbs and plants.

Knowledge was passed down from one generation to another, and so the lore was widely circulated and used. Most country folk knew one herb that was a powerful protection against evil, or a certain flower that produced prophetic dreams, and perhaps a sure-fire love charm or two.

Witches had their own intricate operations of herbal magic, as did the magicians and alchemists. Soon a body of magical knowledge accumulated surrounding the simple herbs that grew beside fast-running streams, in verdant meadows, and high on lonely cliffs.

Many of our ancestors, however, looked to the stars, away from earth, and dreamed of greater things. In racing toward mechanized perfection, humanity became orphaned from the earth, and much of the lore was forgotten.

Fortunately, it was not lost completely. Witches became the keepers of the secrets of the earth; thus, they were looked upon with fear by those who had already turned their backs on the Old Ways. Terror and hatred forced the Witches into hiding, and for centuries the secrets remained untouched.

Today we are experiencing a resurgence of earth awareness. Ecological organizations prosper. Recycling is a booming business. People are turning from chemicals and artificially preserved foods to more healthy fare.

Herbs long unadorned have once again come into their own. But aside from hints and speculation, the magical art of herbalism has largely been left unexplored and unexplained.

In magic, especially herb magic, an herb is a plant prized for its vibrations, or energies. Thus the herbs in this section include seaweed, cacti, trees, fruits and flowers that one might not normally consider to be herbs.

Excerpted from Magical Herbalism: The Secret Craft of the Wise
by Scott Cunningham

Of the Circle

The Circle may be fashioned with garlands of flowers sacred to the gods. Alternately, the flowers should be scattered around the perimeter.

The point candles may be ringed with fresh herbs and flowers suitable to the appropriate element.

Fresh flowers should always be present on the altar or, if none are available, use greens (such as at Yule).

When casting the Circle around a tree, use the fruit, nuts, or flowers of that tree to mark out the Circle.

All of these, of course, are used in addition to the cord or stones.

Of the Fire

The Fire shall be composed of the nine woods:

Rowan
Apple
Elder
Dogwood
Poplar
Juniper
Cedar
Pine
Holly

If these are unavailable, use native wood or oak. Rites run on the seashore should be illuminated with fires of driftwood, collected by the coven prior to the rites.

Of the Covenstead

The plants growing near and around the covenstead are excellent plants to use on the altar during ritual. When the rites must be moved indoors (due to rain or other inclement weather), collect a few sprigs of the plants and bring these into the Circle during ritual.

If the covenstead is indoors, choose an odd-numbered selection of sacred plants to grow there. If they receive little sunlight, move them outdoors occasionally to receive the solar energies. Give them love and energy, and they will aid in your worship and magic.

Of the Coveners

Wear fresh flowers and herbs in your hair and on your body. Crowns of flowers are always appropriate in spring and summer rites, and at all handfastings.

Women may wish to make their necklaces from herbs and seeds, such as tonka beans, whole nutmegs, star anise, acorns, and other seeds and nuts, strung on a natural fiber.

Of the Tools

These are instructions for dedicating the tools prior to the usual consecration.

The Sword or Athame

Rub the blade with fresh basil, rosemary, and oak leaves (or any herbs of Fire) at sunset, outdoors where you will not be disturbed or seen. Lay the sword or athame, point to the South, and sprinkle laurel leaves (preferably fresh) over it, walking deosil thrice around it. Sit before it, facing South, and invoke the God to infuse your sword or athame with his strength. Place your palms on the hilt; grip it tightly, stand, and raise it to the sky, invoking the Goddess to charge your sword or athame with her love.

When the Sun has set, wrap your sword or athame in red silk or cotton cloth and take it home.

The White-Hilted Knife

Go to the forest (or park, garden, etc.). Choose the most beautiful and vibrant plants. Touch the point of the white-hilted knife to these in turn, forging a connection with your knife and the plants (and thus, with the Earth).

Next, being sure that no one sees you, draw an Earth-invoking pentagram on the bare earth, facing North. Now the white-hilted knife may be consecrated.

This dedication should be performed early in the morning.

The Wand

The wand should be selected from a tree of the appropriate type. A general-use wand in the Craft is made of willow, cut during the Full Moon. Other specialized wands can be made, according to the following correspondences:

Apple—Love
Hazel—Wisdom, Divination
Ash—Healing
Birch—Purification
Elder—Evoking and Exorcising Entities
Oak—Solar Workings

or:

Sun: Oak
Moon: Willow
Mars: Hawthorn
Mercury: Hazel
Jupiter: Cedar
Saturn: Poplar
Venus: Apple

The wand should be constructed in the usual way. Just prior to consecration rub the wand with fresh lavender, eucalyptus or mint leaves.

The Pentacle

Place the pentacle on the bare Earth, and cover with dried, crumbled patchouli, parsley, or mistletoe, or fresh jasmine and honeysuckle flowers. Let this remain for forty heartbeats as you sit facing North. Then pick up the pentacle and scatter the herbs or flowers to the four quarters, starting in the North.

(If done indoors, fill a small dish with fresh earth and place the pentacle on this. Proceed as above, throwing the herbs or flowers out the window, or saving them for later scattering outdoors.)

The Censer

Fume pure rosemary or frankincense within the censer prior to its consecration. Do this for at least an hour.

The Cords

Bind with willow.

The Cauldron

Take the cauldron to a stream, a river, lake, or ocean. Dip it into the water and fill it, then set on the water's edge (on both water and earth) and dedicate it to the Goddess, placing your hands on either side of the cauldron, touching the water.

(If inside, perform the rite in the bathtub, after adding a bit of consecrated salt. Let the water be cold or cool.)

The Cup

Anoint the base with gardenia, rose, or violet oil and fill with pure spring water. Then set afloat in the cup a sprig of ivy, a small rose, a fresh gardenia, or some other appropriate herb or flower. Gaze into it and invoke the Goddess to bless the cup.

The Broom

Fashion the broom of an ash staff, birch twigs, and a willow binding. Brush the broom with fresh Water herbs, then bury these with due solemnity.

The Candles

For general rites, add a drop or two of vervain oil to the melted wax prior to making the candles. For Yule, add pine; Beltane, honeysuckle;

Lammas, apple blossom; Hallows, cypress. Use either the oil or herb, whichever is available.

For Full Moon ritual candles, add seven drops of sandalwood oil.

If you must purchase the candles rather than make them, anoint with the specified oils.

The Crystal or Mirror

Rub the mirror on the Full of the Moon with fresh mugwort.

For the crystal, take it outside, hold it up to the Full Moon, and catch the image. Then rub it with fresh mugwort leaves (or dried, if the fresh are unavailable). Repeat for both the crystal and the mirror at least thrice a year.

The Book

Sew into the cover of the Book leaves of the sacred herbs vervain, rue, bay laurel, or others. They must be well-dried and secretly placed by the light of the Full Moon.

Whole dried and pressed catnip or costmary leaves may be used as book marks in the Book.

The Robe

Lay it among sachets filled with lavender, vervain, and cedar when not in use. Sew a bit of rosemary or frankincense into the hem while fashioning it.

Of the Herbs and Plants of the Sabbats

To be used as decorations on the altar and around the Circle.

Samhain

Chrysanthemum, wormwood, apple, hazel, pomegranate, all grains, harvested fruits and nuts, pumpkin.

Yule

Holly, mistletoe, ivy, cedar, bay laurel, juniper, rosemary, pine. Place offerings of oranges, nutmegs, lemons, and whole cinnamon sticks on the Tree.

Candlemas

Snowdrop, rowan, the first flowers of the year.

Spring Equinox

Daffodil, woodruff, gorse, olive, peony, narcissus, all spring flowers.

Beltane

Hawthorn, honeysuckle, St. John's wort.

Summer Solstice

Mugwort, vervain, chamomile, rose, lily, oak, lavender, ivy, yarrow, fern, elder, wild thyme, daisy, carnation.

Lammas

All grains, grapes, heather, blackberries, sloe, crab apples.

Autumn Equinox

Hazel, corn, aspen, acorns, oak sprigs, autumn leaves, wheat stalks, cypress cones, pine cones, harvest gatherings.

Of the Trees of the Sabbats

Samhain: Elder
Yule: Hyssop
Candlemas: Rowan
Spring Equinox: Alder
Beltane: Willow
Summer Solstice: Cedar
Lammas: Holly
Autumn Equinox: Vine

Of Full Moon Rituals

Use all nocturnal, white, or five-petaled flowers, such as the white rose, night-blooming jasmine, carnations, gardenias, lilies, iris—any pleasingly scented flowers which shall call forth the Goddess.

Of Offerings

To the Goddess

Those flowers used in the Full Moon Rituals; blue flowers, those dedicated to Venus or the Moon; rue, vervain, and olive; or others that you see fit.

To the God

All fiery or airy herbs; strong-scented, clean, or citrusy herbs and flowers; yellow or red blooms; cones, seeds, cacti and other stinging herbs; oranges, garlic, cloves, frankincense, and so on.

Also, those specifically dedicated to the gods you are working with.

As the Wicca we will take only that which we need from the green and growing things of the Earth; never failing to attune with the plant before harvesting, nor failing to leave a token of gratitude and respect.

HERE ENDS THIS HERBAL GRIMOIRE

Herbal Recipes
and Secrets

Many Witches combine their magical knowledge of herbs with the medicinal side as well, finding that the two often work in tandem for added power. Herbal cures are frequently boosted with a dash of magic to speed the healing process.

The basis of magical healing is just that, magic. It uses the powers of the herbs fortified and directed by the healer to heal the body directly through the force of magic.

One word of warning: magic is not to be used in the place of professional medical attention. For serious injuries or illnesses, consult a physician as any non-Witch or Witch would do. These remedies are mainly used for lesser maladies.

Excerpted from Magical Herbalism: The Secret Craft of the Wise
by Scott Cunningham

For Coughs

Fill a pot with water, boil a whole lemon for nine minutes, then take out of pot, squeeze out juice, add the same amount of honey, and drink while still hot.

To Sleep

Equal parts:
    Valerian
    Lady's Slipper
    Skullcap

Add one teaspoon to cup of water; let steep nine minutes, strain, and drink. It will be bitter, so you can add honey to help you get it down. The hotter you can drink it, the better. Then rest and relax, and you will fall asleep.

For Digestive Upsets

One teaspoon peppermint to one cup water, steeped, effectively relieves common stomach upsets.

To Clear the Sinuses

Inhale fumes from steeping peppermint or eucalyptus teas, and inhale fumes from eucalyptus oil. Or stand on your head.

For Sunburn

Pour apple cider vinegar or plain black tea, chilled, over the affected areas.

For a Wound

Lay a spider's web over the area until medical attention can be found.

For Poisoning by a Plant

Know the plants in your area, including the poisonous ones and their antidotes. The antidote, by Witch tradition, will be growing nearby any poisonous plant.

If you don't know wild plants, don't eat them. All it takes is one little mistake.

For Headache

Camomile tea rests the head, as does a tea of peppermint and thyme. Or, rub fresh mint leaves on the temples.

Aphrodisia: A Love Drink

1 pinch rosemary
3 pinches thyme
2 teaspoons oriental tea
few pieces orange peel
1 pinch coriander seed
3 mint leaves
5 rose petals
5 lemon leaves
3 pinches nutmeg

Put into teapot. Boil water and add to pot. Sweeten with honey, if desired. Serve hot. Makes 3 cups.

To Repel Flying Insects

Bruise peppermint or alder leaves and rub on skin, clothing.

Herbal Tranquilizer

Brew up a pot of catnip tea and drink it warm, with honey if you wish.

For a Burn

Rub aloe vera (cactus) juice, or administer full-strength Chinese tea (chilled) to the area.

To Prevent Getting a Cold

Drink sassafrass tea while coming out of the cold.

To Stop Smoking

Chew licorice roots when you feel the urge.

To Sleep

Take a small bag and put into it dried rose petals, dried mint, and powdered cloves. To cause sleep, inhale the fragrance.

To Strengthen the Spirits

Go to the garden and pick fresh rosemary, southernwood, marjoram, costmary, and a bit more rosemary. Crush the herbs slightly in your hand and inhale.

To Cure a Cold

Eat a (raw) onion sandwich. Take several eucalyptus berries (green), string on a green thread, and wear around the neck. While collecting berries from the tree, release the cold into the tree. When the cold is gone, bury or throw away eucalyptus necklace.

To Strengthen Virility

Carry an acorn, or a piece of a mandrake root. Eat asparagus and seafood.

Incenses

Incense has smoldered on magicians' altars for at least 5,000 years. It was burned in antiquity to mask odors of sacrificial animals, to carry prayers to the gods, and to create a pleasing environment for humans to meet with deity.

Today, when the age of animal sacrifices among most Western magicians is long past, the reasons for incense use are varied. It is burned during magic to promote ritual consciousness, the state of mind necessary to rouse and direct personal energy. This is also achieved through the use of magical tools, by standing before the candle-bewitched altar, and by intoning chants and symbolic words.

When burned prior to magical workings, fragrant smoke also purifies the altar and the surrounding area of negative, disturbing vibrations. Though such a purification isn't usually necessary, it, once again, helps create the appropriate mental state necessary for the successful practice of magic.

Specially formulated incenses are burned to attract specific energies to the magician and to aid her or him in charging personal power with the ritual's goal, eventually creating the necessary change.

Incense, in common with all things, possesses specific vibrations. The magician chooses the incense for magical use with these vibrations in mind. If performing a healing ritual, she or he burns a mixture composed of herbs that promote healing.

When the incense is smoldered in a ritual setting, it undergoes a transformation. The vibrations, no longer trapped in their physical form, are released into the environment. Their energies, mixing with those of the magician, speed out to effect the changes necessary to the manifestation of the goal.

Not all incense formulas are strictly for magical use. Some are smoldered in thanks or offering to various aspects of deity, just as juniper was burned to Inanna 5,000 years ago in Sumer. Other blends are designed to enhance Wiccan rituals.

Excerpted from The Complete Book of Incense, Oils & Brews
by Scott Cunningham

Sabbat Incense

Bay Laurel
Fennel
Thyme
Pennyroyal
Solomon's Seal
Rue
Wormwood
Vervain
Camomile
Hemp
Frankincense
Myrrh
Benzoin

The last three ingredients should be the bulk of the mixture. Compound while the Moon is waxing.

Esbat Incense

Storax
Camphor
Orris
Thyme
White Poppy
Wood Aloe
Calamus
Rosebuds
Cinnamon
Coriander
Frankincense
Myrrh
Benzoin

Mix on Full Moon.

Circle Incense

Frankincense
Myrrh
Benzoin
Cinnamon
Rose petals
Vervain
Rosemary
Sandalwood
Bay Laurel

Equal Parts. Mix in waxing Moon. Use for general magical rites, rites of worship, or when no other incense is called for or available.

Compound Planetary

Frankincense ☉
Orris ☽
Lavender ☿
Rose petals ♀
Dragon's Blood ♂
Cinquefoil ♃
Solomon's Seal ♄

Mix during the waxing Moon.

COMPOUND PLANETARY

Frankincense-☼
Orris-☊
Lavender-☿
Rose Petals- ♀
Dragon's Blood-♂
Cinquefoil-♃
Solomon's Seal-♄

Mix during the waxing Moon.

Planetary Incenses

Sun

Frankincense
Cinnamon
Bay Laurel
Galangal
Mistletoe
Wine
Honey

Moon

Orris
Juniper Berries
Calamus
Camphor
Lotus Oil

Mercury

Sandalwood
Lavender
Gum Mastic (or Benzoin)

Venus

Rosebuds
Red Sandalwood
Benzoin
Patchouli

Mars

Dragon's Blood
Grains of Paradise (or Cayenne Pepper)
Black Pepper
Cardamom
Cloves
Cassia (or cinnamon)

Jupiter

Cedar
Vetivert
Rosewood
Saffron
Olive Oil

Saturn

Ambrette
Myrrh
Dittany of Crete
Cypress Oil

Elemental Incenses

Air

Mastic
Lavender
Mistletoe
Benzoin
Wormwood

Water

Myrrh
Benzoin
Civet
Ambergris
Aloe (Aloe Vera)
Camphor
Lotus Oil

Fire

Frankincense
Musk
Dragon's Blood
Red Sandalwood
Saffron

Earth

Dittany of Crete
Patchouli
Storax
Salt
Cypress Oil
Narcissus Oil

Exorcism Incense

Bay Laurel
Solomon's Seal
Avens
Mugwort
Yarrow
St. John's Wort
Angelica
Rosemary
Basil

Mix during the waning Moon.

Consecration Incense

Wood Aloe
Storax
Mace
Benzoin

Fire of Azrael

Cedar
Sandalwood
Juniper

Mix during waxing Moon. For scrying, light a fire of driftwood near the sea. When it dies down, throw the incense on the coals. Lie down and scry. May also be used as incense at home.

Scrying Incense

Mugwort
Wormwood

Equal parts. Mix and burn a small amount prior to scrying.

Divination Incense

Cloves, 1 part
Chicory, 3 parts
Cinquefoil, 1 part

Mix while Moon is waxing.

Vision Incense

Bay Laurel
Frankincense
Damiana
Hemp

Sight Incense

Gum Mastic (or Benzoin)
Rush Roots
Cinnamon

Musk or Ambrette
Juniper
Sandalwood
Ambergris
Hemp
Patchouli

Compound during waxing Moon.

Healing Incense

Cloves
Nutmeg
Lemon Balm
Poppy Seed
Cedar
Honeysuckle Oil
Almond Oil

Love Incense

Lavender
Dragon's Blood
Myrtle
Rosebuds
Orris
Musk Oil or Ambrette
Patchouli

Protection Incense

Frankincense		Frankincense
Wood Betony	or	Sandalwood
Dragon's Blood		Rosemary

Rosemary or frankincense alone may be burned. Use as necessary, morning, noon, and night.

Intensified Protection

Bay Laurel
Avens
Mugwort
Yarrow
Rosemary
St. John's Wort
Angelica
Basil
Juniper Berries

Study Incense

Cinnamon
Rosemary
Benzoin

Burn small amount while studying.

Offertory Incense

Rose Petals
Vervain
Cinnamon
Myrrh
Frankincense

Burn while honoring the God and Goddess.

Altar Incense

Frankincense
Cinnamon
Myrrh

Burn to cleanse the altar.

Kernunnos Incense

Pine
Sandalwood
Civet
Valerian
Musk
Cinnamon
Frankincense

To honor him. Use but a pinch of valerian root unless you wish a very strongly-scented incense.

House Consecration Incense

Dill
Frankincense
Wood Betony
Dragon's Blood
Sandalwood
Rose
Geranium Oil
Myrrh

Burn in your new home before moving in, or to cleanse your home. This is traditionally burned in the spring.

Full Moon Incense

Sandalwood
Frankincense
Camphor

Use just a pinch of camphor. Burn on the Full Moon.

"For Emergencies" Incense

Asafoetida
Garlic flowers
Frankincense
Myrrh
Cayenne Pepper
Grains of Paradise
Rue
Dragon's Blood
Rosemary

Burn only in cases of extraordinary psychic danger. Do not inhale for pro-longed periods. Keep a little in the Circle of Stones for emergencies.

To Bring Rain

Heather
Fern
Henbane

Burn together out of doors to attract rain.

Nine Woods Incense

Rowan (or Ash)
Apple
Elder
Dogwood
Poplar
Juniper
Cedar
Pine
Holly

Equal parts, powdered. Use in indoor rites in place of the balefire.

Full Moon Ritual Incense

Dried Gardenia blossoms
Frankincense
Ground Orris root

Crush together in the mortar on the Full Moon. Use for lunar rites.

Meditation Incense

Bay Laurel
Sandalwood
Damiana

Burn small amount prior to meditating.

Drawing Incense

Jasmine
Violet
Lavender

Draws helpful spirits, assistance in all important matters, good luck.

Hermes Incense

Lavender
Mastic
Cinnamon

For concentration and creativity.

Aphrodite Incense

Cinnamon
Cedar
Violet Oil

For love rites.

Uncrossing Incense

Dragon's Blood
Frankincense
Rosemary

For banishing evil.

Holy Water

Collect any nine sacred plants and herbs and let set in rain or spring water for three days. Strain. Sprinkle with an asperger. The asperger should be rue if for healing, laurel if for protection, rosemary if for exorcism. Attach a sprig of the herb to a small twig with thread for your asperger. Dip the herb into the holy water and sprinkle.

Herbal Pillows

Dream Pillow: Mugwort, or Lemon Balm, Costmary, Rose, Mint, Cloves
Nightmare Cure: Anise seed
Melancholy Cure: Thyme
Easy Sleep: Stuff a small pillowcase with fresh peppermint. Refill every
night, as the herb does not last.

To Strengthen the Eyesight

Gather the dew from the fennel or celandine and place on the lids.

True Dream

At night, grind a hazelnut and walnut together. Add a pinch of nutmeg. Mix with butter and brown sugar to form many small pellets. Eat seven pellets one hour before retiring to produce true dreams!

Ritual Bath Salts

To one cup plain salt, add several drops of the oil that possesses those vibrations you wish to bring into your life. Food coloring may be added to intensify the finished bath salt.

Herbs

Sacred Herbs of the Goddesses

Aphrodite	Olive, Cinnamon, Daisy, Cypress, Quince
Aradia	Rue, Vervain
Artemis	Silver Fir, Cypress, Cedar, Hazel, Myrtle, Willow
Ashtoreth	Cypress, Myrtle
Astarte	Alder
Athena	Olive
Bast	Catnip
Cailleach	Corn
Cardea	Hawthorn
Ceres	Willow, Wheat, Poppy, Leek, Narcissus
Circe	Willow
Cybele	Acorn, Myrrh, Pinecone
Demeter	Corn, Barley, Pennyroyal, Myrrh, Rose
Diana	Birch, Wormwood, Dittany, Hazel, Beech, Fir
Druantia	Fir
Eos	Saffron
Freya	Primrose, Maidenhair, Myrrh, Strawberry
Hathor	Myrtle, Sycamore, Mandrake, Coriander
Hecate	Willow, Henbane, Aconite, Yew, Mandrake, Cyclamen, Mint
Hera	Pomegranate, Myrrh
Hulda	Flax, Rose, Hellebore, Elder

Iris	Wormwood
Ishtar	All grains
Isis	Heather, Corn, Absinthe, Barley, Myrrh, Rose
Juno	Lily, Crocus, Asphodel, Quince, Pomegranate, Vervain, Iris, Lettuce
Minerva	Olive
Nephthys	Myrrh
Nuit	Sycamore
Persephone	Narcissus, Willow, Pomegranate
Proserpine	Daffodil
Rhea	Myrrh
Venus	Cinnamon, Daisy, Heather, Anemone, Apple, Poppy, Violet, Marjoram, Maidenhair Fern, Carnation, Aster, Vervain, Myrtle, Orchid, Cedar

Sacred Herbs of the Gods

Adonis	Myrrh, Corn, Rose, Fennel, Lettuce
Aesculapius	Laurel
Apollo	Laurel, Leek, Hyacinth, Heliotrope, Cornel, Bay, Frankincense
Ares	Buttercup
Attis	Pine
Bacchus	Grape, Ivy, Fig, Beech
Bran	Alder, Grain
Cupid	Sugar Cane, White Violets, Red Rose
Dadga	Oak
Dianus	Fig
Dionysius	Fig, Vine and Grapes, Pine, Corn, Pomegranate, all wild and cultivated trees, toadstools, and mushrooms
Dis	Cypress
Eros	Red Rose

Gwydion	Ash
Helios	Sunflower, Heliotrope
Hercules	Apple (fruit), Poplar, Beech
Horus	Horehound, Lotus
Hypnos	Poppy
Jove	Pink, Cassia, Houseleek, Carnation
Jupiter	Aloe, Agrimony, Sage, Oak, Mullein, Beech, Houseleek, Palm, Violet, Gorse
Kernunnos	Heliotrope, Laurel, Sunflower, Oak, Orange
Mars	Aloe, Dogwood, Buttercup, Dog Grass, Vervain
Mercury	Cinnamon, Mulberry, Hazel, Willow
Mithras	Cypress
Osiris	Acacia, Vine and Grapes, Corn, Ivy, Tamarisk, Cedar
Pan	Fig, Fir, Reed, Ferns
Pluto	Cypress, Mint
Poseidon	Pine, Ash
Ra	Frankincense, Myrrh
Rimmon (Adonis)	Pomegranate
Saturn	Fig, Bramble
Tammuz	Corn, Pomegranate
Thor	Thistle, Houseleek, Vervain, Hazel, Ash, Birch, Rowan, Acorn, Pomegranate
Woden	Ash
Zeus	Oak, Olive, Pine, Aloe, Parsley, Sage, Wheat

Herbal Code

In old recipes, strange ingredients are often called for. Here's what is really being requested:

Brains: congealed gum from a Cherry Tree

Eyes: Eyebright or Daisy

Blood: Elder Sap

Fingers: Cinquefoil

Hair: Maidenhair Fern

Skin of a Man: Fern

Unicorn Horn: True Unicorn Root

Bull's Blood: Horehound

Piss: Dandelion

Bloody Fingers: Foxglove

Tongue of Dog: Hound's Tongue

Dragon's Scales: Bistort leaves

Snake: Bistort

Ear of an Ass: Comfrey

Heart: Walnut

Ears of a Goat: St. John's Wort

Skull: Skullcap

Worms: Gnarled, thin roots of a local tree

Lion's Tooth: Dandelion

Tooth or Teeth: Pine Cones

Corpse Candles: Mullein

A *Dead Man:* Ash root, carved into a crude human shape.

Hand: the unexpanded frond from a male fern, used to make the true hand of glory, which was nothing more than a candle made of regular wax mixed with fern. Used in old ceremonies.

When these animals are called for, use the herb instead:

Sheep: Dandelion

Dog: Couchgrass

Lamb: Lamb's Lettuces

Cat: Catnip

Rat: Valerian

Weasel: Rue

Nightingale: Hop

Cuckoo: Orchis, Plantain

Hawk: Hawkweed

Linnets: Eyebright

Woodpeckers: Peony

Blue Jay: Bay Laurel

Snake: Fennel or Bistort

Frog: Cinquefoil

Toad: Sage

Lizard: Calamint

When a sacrifice is called for, it means that you should bury an egg. **Never** does it mean to kill any living thing!

Herbal Code

The part called for in a recipe means the part of the herb to be used, as follows:

The head: is the flower

The paw, foot, leg, or scale: is the leaf

The tooth: is the leaf, seed pod

The guts: are the roots and stalk

The tail: is the stem

The tongue: is the petal

The privates: are the seeds

The hair: is the dried, stringy herb

The eye: is the inner part of a blossom

The heart: is a bud, or a big seed.

These plants are often called for in old recipes. Note that they are plants, and not animals!

Crowfoot	Duck's Meat	Goat's Foot	Dragon's Blood
Dog's Teeth	Hare's Foot	Hen and Chickens	Cat's Foot
Hare's Ear	Hart's Tongue	Horse Foot	Adder's Tongue
Mouse Ear	Horse Tail	Horse Hoof	Lion's Tail
Frog's Foot	Kidneywort	Ladies Thumb	
Cat's Tail	Bear's Foot	Lion's Mouth	

Bird's Foot	Goatsbeard	Ox Tongue
Crab's Claws	Bird's Eye	Robin's Eyes
Dove's Foot	Bird's Tongue	Turtle's Head
Colt's Tail	Bull's Foot	Fox's Tongue
Coltsfoot	Dragon's Claw	Snake's Tongue

All plants named in the common language 'the Devil's this' or 'Old Man's that' are in actuality sacred to the God. All plants named 'Our Lady's so-and-so' or 'Mary's such' are sacred and dedicated to the Goddess.

Of the Places Where Plants and Herbs Are to Be Found

Fields

Vervain, Mugwort, Mercury, Cinquefoil, Jack by the Hedge, Wild Tansy, Knot Grass, Wild Orange, Flaxweed, Houndstongue, Shepherd's Purse, Yarrow, Knapweed, Ragwort, Scabious, Dandelion, Lady's Bedstraw, Docks, Daisies, Wild Carrots, Mullein, Trefoil, Earthnuts, Horehound, etc.

Amongst Grain

Bluebottles, Poppies, Restharrow, Fumitory, Shepherd's Needle, Mayweed, Cockle, Corn Marigold, Pimpernel, Cow-Parsnip, Bindweed, Sow-Thistle

Woods

Woodspurge, Tormentil, Agrimony, Ladies Mantle, St. John's Wort, Wood Betony, Wood Sorrel, Woodruff, Satyrions, Moonwort, Cistus, Milkwort

Meadows

Marsh Marigold, Meadsweet, Burnet, Coxcomb, Saxifrage, Meadow Rhubarb, Lousewort

Housetops

Houseleek, Stonecrop, Herb Robert, Seengreen

Bogs

Horsemint, Cottongrass, Pennyroyal, Butterwort, Bucksbean, Sun Dew, Stinking Horsetails, Valerian

River Sides

Valerian, Comfrey, Sneezewort, Watercress, all the Mints, Allheal, the Great Dock, Water Hemp, Willow-Weed, Water Hemlock, Water-Betony, etc.

Banks of Rivers

Water Lily, Water Milfoil, Frogbit, Calthrobs, Burnweed, Water Plantains, Arrowhead, Water Parsley, all types of Figs, Bulrushes, Reeds

Ditches

Ducksmeat, Brooklime, Water Crowfoot, Watercress, Water Parsnip, Water Horehound, Water Scorpion Grass, Horsemint

Walls

Maidenhair, Wall Bugloss, Whitelow Grass, Polypod, Rocket, Wall-flowers, Morning Glory, Pellitory, Rue

Positive, Masculine, and Stimulating Herbs

These are excellent adjuncts to spells and operations involving men, strength, will-power, endurance, material objects, employers and employees, intelligence and study, rulers and political leaders, sex, money, and so on. As with any operation of magic, however, avoid manipulation of other beings and never use any of these herbs internally.

Vervain	Frankincense	St. John's Wort
Nettle	Rosemary	Mustard
Vanilla	Grains of Paradise	All-Spice
Anise	Rose Geranium	Feverfew
Ambrette	Goldenrod	Carnation
Ginger	Bay Laurel	Hawthorn
Thyme	Hyssop	Thistle
Marigold	Spearmint	Myrrh

Patchouli	Yarrow	Damiana
Eucalyptus	Garlic	Woodruff
Dill	Dragon's Blood	Clove
Saffron	Cinnamon	Pine
Celandine	Oak	Pennyroyal
Holly	Heliotrope	Periwinkle
Coriander	*Tobacco	Cacti
*Mandrake	Curry Leaf	Hibiscus
Sunflower	Mullein	

Herbs marked with an asterisk (*) are dangerous, Do not take (or inhale fumes) internally

POSITIVE, MASCULINE AND STIMULATING HERBS

These are excellent adjuncts to spells and operations involving men, strength, will-power, endurance, material objects, employers and employees, intelligence and study, rulers and policital leaders, sex, money, and so on.

As with any operation of magic, however, avoid manipulation of other beings and never use any of these herbs internally.

Vervain	Frankincense
St. John's Wort	Nettle
Rosemary	Mustard
Vanilla	Grains of Paradise
All-Spice	Anise
Rose Geranium	Feverfew
Ambrette	Goldenrod
Carnation	Ginger
Bay Laurel	Hawthorn
Thyme	Hyssop
Thistle	Marigold
Spearmint	Myrrh
Patchouli	Yarrow
Damiana	Eucalyptus
Garlic	Woodruff
Dill	Dragon's Blood
Clove	Saffron
Cinnamon	Pine
Celandine	Oak
Pennyroyal	Holly
Heliotrope	Periwinkle
Coriander	☿Tobacco
Cacti	☿Mandrake
Curry Leaf	Hibiscus
Sunflower	
Mullein	

*herbs marked ☿ are dangerous.
Do not take (or inhale fumes) internally

Negative, Feminine, and Relaxing Herbs

These are herbs to use in operations and spells involving women, sleep, prophecy and divination, visions, love and sex, the emotions, spirituality, healing, handfastings, and fertility.

Do not take internally or inhale fumes! Herbs marked with asterisk (*) are particularly dangerous.

Hops	Plumeria
Scullcap	Gardenia
Dittany of Crete	Cedar
Kava Kava	Night-Blooming Cereus
Lady's Slipper	Motherwort
Valerian	Primrose
Poppy	Orris
Chamomile	Magnolia
Bergamot	Cucumber
Catnip	*Henbane
Hyacinth	*Deadly Nightshade
Lavender	Tonka
Meadowsweet	Tormentil
Lettuce	Cypress
Jasmine	Grapes
Hemp	Camphor
Willow	Kelp
Primrose	Lotus
Nutmeg	Water Lily
Peppermint	Water Cress
Passion Flower	Loosestrife
Tuberose	Lovage

Neutral or Hermaphroditic Herbs

These are the herbs to use in operations of the intellect, to cool down undue ardor or passion of all kinds, for self-control (such as when dieting). They bring balance into an unbalanced life. Do not take internally or inhale fumes.

Grapefruit	Lemon
Orange	Marjoram
Lemon Verbena	Lemon Balm
Lemon Grass	Tangerine
Raspberry	

Herbs, Plants, Flowers of Protection

Elder (berries, bark, twigs, leaves)

Vervain

St. John's wort

* Rue

Juniper

* Mistletoe

Pimpernel

Cyclamen

Angelica

Snapdragon

Betony

Avens

Dill

Flax

Trefoil (three-leaved clover)

Bay Laurel

Rowan

Marjoram

* Ash twigs, berries

Houseleek

Mugwort

Elder (berries, bark,
Vervain
St. John's Wort
♀ Rue
Juniper
♀ Mistletoe
Pimpernel
Cyclamen
Angelica
Snapdragon
Betony
Avens
Dill
Flax
Trefoil (three-leaved
Bay Laurel
Rowan
Marjoram
♀ Ash twigs, berries
Houseleek
Mugwort
Elecampane

Elecampane
Rosemary
Mullein
Lady's Slipper
Asafoetida
* Bittersweet
Fennel
Fumitory
Horehound
Periwinkle
Balm of Gilead
Basil
Peony
Garlic
Onion

Rosemary
Mullein
Lady's Slipper
Asafoetida
℞ Bittersweet
Fennel
Fumitory
Horehound
Periwinkle
Balm of Gilead
Basil
Peony
Garlic
Onion.

Use in the standard ways
for protection.

Use in the standard ways for protection.

Herbs marked with an asterisk (*) are dangerous. Do not take internally or inhale fumes.

Herbs, Plants, Flowers of Healing

Amaranth
Anemone
Cinnamon
Saffron
Spearmint
Peppermint
Sage
Eucalyptus
Hops
Red Geranium
Carnation
Lavender
Narcissus
Sandalwood
Violet
Rue
Rosemary
Myrrh
Rose
Balm of Gilead
Thistles

Use in candle magic, healing sachets, incenses, and bath bags, and so on. But ever remember, prevention is better than curing!

Herbs, Plants, Flowers of Exorcism

Solomon's Seal

Avens

Bay Laurel

Garlic Flowers

Onion Flowers

Thistle

Aloes Wood

Honesty

Juniper

* Black Hellebore

Peony

Mugwort

Elder

Nettle

Yarrow

St. John's Wort

Garlic

Angelica

Marjoram

Sloe

Rosemary

Basil

Asafoetida

Frankincense

Myrrh

```
       Solomon's Seal
       Avens
       Bay Laurel
       Garlic Flowers
       Onion Flowers
       Thistle
       Aloes Wood
       Honesty
       Juniper
      ☿Black Hellebore
       Peony
       Mugwort
       Elder
       Nettle
       Yarrow
       St. John's Wort
       Garlic
       Angelica
       Marjoram
       Sloe
       Rosemary
       Basil
       Asafoetida
       Frankincense
       Myrrh
```

Herbs marked with an asterisk (*) are dangerous, Do not take internally or inhale fumes.

When using such ingredients in incenses, use small amounts, especially with those marked as dangerous, and never inhale the smoke. Always leave the area until the incense has gone out and the smoke is well cleared. To facilitate this, and also because it's good magical practice, when using exorcism incense in a dwelling, open all doors and windows. If you're afraid of burglars, the smell alone should keep them away, but you can watch the place too.

Herbs, Plants, Flowers that Bind

Myrrh

Black Poppy Seeds

Elderberries

Periwinkle, the juice

* Rue

Sorrel

Hawthorn

Juniper

* Yew

* Nightshade

Cacti

* Henbane

* Datura

* Hemlock

Nettle

Thistle

```
    Myrrh
    Black Poppy Seeds
    Elderberries
    Periwinkle - the juice
  ♀ Rue
    Sorrel
    Hawthorn
    Juniper
  ♀ Yew
  ♀ Nightshade
    Cacti
   ♀Henbane
   ♀Datura
   ♀Hemlock
    Nettle
    Thistle
```

Herbs marked with an asterisk (*) are dangerous. Do not take internally or inhale fumes.

Binding magic is sometimes necessary, but it is very dangerous and can lead to serious consequences. Consult your gods, your teacher, and your fellow Wiccans, as well as your own conscience, before embarking on binding magic. It is not to be done lightly. Only in the time of greatest need can it be used.

Mind the words of your oath!

Herbs, Plants, Flowers of Love

Meadowsweet	Southernwood
Mandrake	Satyrion
Jasmine	Violet
Bergamot	Periwinkle
Rose	Orris Root
Basil	Vervain
Lavender	Tormentil
Apple	Rosemary
Yarrow	Dragon's Blood
Lemon Balm	Myrtle
Orange	Bachelor's Buttons
Cumin	Coriander
Caraway	Elecampane
Pink Geranium	Lovage
* Kava Kava	Tonka Beans
Marjoram	Endive
Aster	Balm of Gilead
* Henbane	

To encourage love to come into one's life. Herbs marked with an asterisk (*) are dangerous. Do not take internally or inhale fumes.

HERBS, PLANTS, FLOWERS OF LOVE

Meadowsweet
Southernwood
Mandrake
Satyrion
Jasmine
Violet
Bergamot
Periwinkle
Rose
Orris Root
Basil
Vervain
Lavender
Tormentil
Apple
Rosemary
Yarrow
Dragon's Blood
Lemon Balm
Myrtle
Orange
Bachelor's Buttons
Cumin
Coriander
Caraway
Elecampane
Pink Geranium
Lovage
♀ Kava Kava
Tonka Beans
Marjoram
Endive
Aster
Balm of Gilead
⚥ Henbane

To encourage love to come into one's life.

Herbs, Plants, Flowers of Divination

Mugwort
Ash leaves
Bay Laurel
Bistort
Eyebright
Marigold
Goldenrod
Star Anise
Thyme
Wormwood
Yarrow
Hemp
Patchouli
Rosebuds
Anise
Heliotrope
Lilac
Acacia
Anise
Cinnamon
* Nutmeg
Chicory
Cinquefoil
Gum Mastic
Sandalwood

Herbs marked with an asterisk (*) are dangerous. Do not take large amounts internally or inhale fumes.

Incenses, baths, etc. For incenses, burn small amounts only, and prior to the operation itself.

HERBS, PLANTS, FLOWERS OF DIVINATION

Mugwort
Ash Leaves
Bay laurel
Bistort
Eyebright
Marigold
Goldenrod
Star Anise
Thyme
Wormwood
Yarrow
Hemp
Patchouli
Rosebuds
Anise
Heliotrope
Lilac
Acacia
Anise
Cinnamon
♀ Nutmeg
Chicory
Cinquefoil
Gum Mastic
Sandalwood

Incenses, baths, etc. For incenses, burn small amounts
only, and prior to the operation itself.

Herbs, Plants, Flowers of Lust

Rosemary	* Kava Kava
Coriander	Cumin
Carrots	Endive
Celery	Poppy (seed)
Dill	Peppermint
Caraway	Capers
Ginger	Pine
Elecampane	Almond
Mint	Pimento
Saffron	Sesame
Tarragon	Vanilla
Clove	Ginger Blossoms
Lavender	Musk
Patchouli	Tuberose
Vanilla	Violet
Cinnamon	Tomato
Cocoa Bean	Banana
Avocado	Papaya
Cardamom	Apple

Herbs marked with an asterisk (*) are dangerous. Do notT take internally or inhale fumes.

Careful!

HERBS, PLANTS, FLOWERS OF LUST

Rosemary
⚥ Kava Kava
Coriander
Cumin
Carrots
Endive
Celery
Poppy (seed)
Dill
Peppermint
Caraway
Capers
Ginger
Pine
Elecampane
Almond
Mint
Pimento
Saffron
Sesame
Tarragon
Vanilla
Clove
Ginger Blossoms
Lavender
Musk
Patchouli
Tuberose   Banana
Vanilla   Avacado
Violet   Banana
Cinnamon   Cardamom
Tomato   Apple
Cocoa Bean   Papaya

Careful!

Lightning Herbs

Holly

Fern

Parsley

Hawthorn

Elder

Gooseberry

Houseleek

Mistletoe

Oak

Rowan

Use in anti-lightning protective rituals, mixtures.

Herbs, Plants, Flowers of Fertility

Asparagus

Acorn

Cucumber

Hazel

Fig

Pine Cone

Poppy (seed)

Apple

Eat or use in rituals designed to increase your own fertility, or use as symbols of fertility during celebrations.

Oils

It has become quite popular to use essential oils for magical purposes. Such practices, often thought of as being ancient, do indeed date back thousands of years in one form or another; but not until recently were the array of true and synthetic botanical oils available for ritual purposes.

Scented oils were used in antiquity. These were created by heating fragrant plant materials in oil or fat. The plant's scent was transferred to the oil and thus was fragrant.

Many people tell me they want to make their own oils. Unfortunately, this is a difficult process. Why? Here are a few reasons:

- It requires a large investment in equipment.
- It requires a large amount of fresh plant materials.
- The process must be carefully carried out to exacting standards.
- Often the results aren't worth the investment of time and money.

There are a few plant oils that can be extracted at home without much difficulty. For the rest, simply buy and blend high quality oils for ritual use.

It is best to use only genuine, authentic essential oils in magic. These contain the sum of the plant's magical energies and so are the most effective. True, they aren't cheap, but they last longer because only small amounts are necessary.

There is no magic secret for blending and mixing magical oils. Here's the basic method:

- Assemble the essential oils (and bouquets) called for in the recipe.
- In a clean, sterilized jar add ⅛ cup of a vegetable oil. I've found jojoba works the best because it isn't truly an oil, but a form of liquid wax, it never becomes rancid and can be kept for longer periods of time.
- Using an eye dropper, add the oils in recommended proportions.
- Swirl the essential oils into the base oil, don't stir. Gently rotate the oil clockwise.
- Finally, store all oils away from heat, light, and moisture.

Excerpted from The Complete Book of Incense, Oils & Brews
by Scott Cunningham

Sabbat Oil

Vervain		Basil
Cinquefoil	or	Cinquefoil
Parsley		Poplar buds
		Sweet Flag

Soot was often added in past times. Mix well and let steep for three weeks, changing the herbs every three days. Strain and expose to the Moon three nights, during her waxing.

Use for the Sabbat, anointing the traditional thirteen points:
Soles of the feet
Bends of the knees
Base of the spine
Genitals
Wrists
Over the heart
The breasts
Under the chin
The forehead

Musk, carnation, or frankincense oil is usually added to improve the scent, should it be lacking. A few more modern recipes are:

Olive Oil		Patchouli
Musk	or	Musk
Cinnamon		Carnation

Admission Oil

Frankincense
Myrrh
Sandalwood

Combine the essences. Place in a bottle and leave for one lunar month.
Anoint the seeker/candidate according to tradition.

Solar Oil

Cinnamon
Frankincense
Galangal

Use to invoke the masculine forces within.

Lunar Oil

Gardenia
Jasmine
Lotus

Use to invoke the feminine forces within.

Far Sight Oil

Acacia
Cassia
Anise

Wear to aid clairvoyance.

Healing Oil

Sandalwood
Carnation
Rosemary

Mix, pour into green glass jar and set for seven days where it will receive light of the Sun by day and that of the Moon by night.

Four Winds Oils

East Wind, the wind of intelligence: Lavender
South Wind, the wind of passion and change: Musk
West Wind, the wind of love and the emotions: Rose
North Wind, the wind of riches and stability: Honeysuckle

Prophetic Dream Oil

½ cup olive oil
1 pinch cinnamon
1 pinch nutmeg
1 teaspoon anise

Heat until warm but not hot; strain. Apply to forehead and temples before sleep.

Protection Oil

Rosemary
Rose Geranium
Cypress

Use as needed. Blend during the waxing Moon.

Venus Oil

Jasmine
Rose } base, equal parts

Ylang Ylang
Gardenia } a few drops
Violet

Your own link—a drop

Lavender
Musk } scant drop each

This formula is for *women only*. Anoint the genitals, base of the spine, palms of the hands, and breasts.

(Note: link = blood, sweat, semen, etc.)

VENUS OIL

Jasmine
Rose } base, equal parts

Ylang Ylang
Gardenia } a few drops
Violet

your own link - a drop

Lavender
Musk } scant drop each

This formula is for women only. Anoint the genitals, base of the spine, palms of the hands and breasts.

(Note: link = blood, sweat, semen, etc.)

Satyr Oil

Musk
Patchouli } base, equal parts

Civet
Ambergris } a few drops
Cinnamon

Your own link—a drop

Allspice
Carnation } scant drop each

Prepare according to above instructions, starting with the musk and patchouli.

This formula is for *men only*. Anoint the genitals, palms of the hands and base of the spine.

SATYR OIL

Musk
Patchouli } base, equal parts

Civet
Ambergris } a few drops
Cinnamon

your own link - a drop

Allspice
Carnation } scant drop each

Prepare according to above instructions, starting with the musk and patchouli.
This formula is for <u>men only</u>. Anoint the genitals, palms of the hands and base of the spine.

Essential Oils

For convenience these oils are listed by their particular powers. Use these lists for substitutions in recipes or for formulating your own.

Some of the oils are listed in more than one category simply because they are possessed of numerous powers.

Concentration

Honeysuckle
Lilac
Rosemary

Courage

Rose Geranium
Musk
Iris

Fertility

Musk
Vervain

Harmony

Basil
Gardenia
Lilac
Narcissus

Healing

Carnation
Eucalyptus
Lotus
Myrrh
Narcissus
Rosemary
Sandalwood

Violet
Myrrh

High Vibrations

Acacia
Cinnamon
Clove
Frankincense
Jasmine
Myrrh
Sandalwood

Love

Clove
Gardenia
Jasmine
Orris

Magnetic Oils

Women wear:
  Ambergris
  Gardenia
  Ginger Flower
  Jasmine
  Tuberose
  Violet

Men Wear:
  Bay
  Civet
  Musk
  Patchouli
  Vetivert

Meditation

Acacia

Hyacinth

Jasmine

Magnolia

Myrrh

Nutmeg

Money

Bayberry

Honeysuckle

Mint

Vervain

New Beginnings

New-mown Hay

Passion

Cinnamon

Cassia

Clove

Lavender—arouses men

Musk—arouses men

Neroli—arouses men

Patchouli

Stephanoti—arouses women

Vanilla

Violet—arouses women

Peace

Benzoin

Gardenia

Magnolia

Rose

Tuberose

Power

Carnation
Rosemary
Vanilla

Protection

Cypress
Myrrh
Patchouli
Rose
Geranium
Rosemary
Rue
Violet

Psychic Powers

Acacia
Anise
Cassia
Heliotrope
Lilac
Mimosa
Tuberose

Recalling Past Lives

Lilac
Sandalwood

Spiritual Vibrations (for spiritual development)

Heliotrope
Lotus
Magnolia

Vitalizing

Allspice
Carnation
Rosemary
Vanilla

Ritual Bath

Vervain
Garden Mint
Basil
Thyme
Fennel
Lavender
Rosemary
Hyssop
Valerian

Use slightly less of Valerian; otherwise, equal parts. Mix and put into bath bags during the Moon's increase. Tie with red drawstring and use one for every bath. Make up several so that you have a good stock on hand.

The Bath

Fill the tub with warm water, add half a handful sea salt, a little cider vinegar, and the bath bag full of herbs. Let the herbs color the water. Relax and drain yourself of tenseness, dirt, psychic garbage. Scrub your skin with the bag to release the oils inside the herbs and to wake yourself. Drain the water and step out refreshed, ready to perform a work of worship, attunement, or magic.

Magical Lore, Spells, and Rituals

A spell is a magical ritual. It's usually nonreligious in nature and often involves the use of symbols or symbolic actions and words. It's a specific series of movements, use of tools, and inner processes (such as visualization) to create a specific manifestation.

A spell is a spell is a spell. Old spells are no more effective than new spells. But to manifest your need, the spell must be designed to do three things:

a) Raise personal power (and in natural magic, to unite it with earth power).

b) Program this energy (through visualization).

c) Release the energy.

This book is filled with spells of all types. Each is designed to accomplish these three things, but they need the magician's help. A spell is truly magical only in the hands of a magician. Once you've started practicing magic, you are a magician.

Excerpted from Earth, Air, Fire & Water *by Scott Cunningham*

The Places to Perform Magic

The places best fitted for magic making are those which are concealed, removed, and separated from the places of men. Desolate and uninhabited regions are most appropriate, such as the borders of lakes, forests, islands, mountains, caves, grottos, and deserts. Lightning-struck trees, ancient earthworks, standing stones, and a crossroads where three roads meet, Diana's domain, are also appropriate.

But if such places are remote, or if some force hinders the performance of magic in these places, your house, or garden, or indeed, any place, provided it has been purified and consecrated with the necessary ceremonies, will be fit in the sight of the gods.

These arts should be carried out at night; this is the time of greatest lunar power, and is also a symbol that it is just and right to hide them from the sight of the foolish, the ignorant, and the profane.

The Places of Magic

The desert is the place of extremes; it is a place of masculine, powerful, intellectual, philosophical magic. As such, it is excellent for meditation, for visualization, for attuning yourself to the winds and the sun and fire. Of course it is fine for calling forth the salamanders and sylphs and the God.

The seashore is the place of feminine energy, where sea and land, the two female elements, meet. Here is the place for spiritual growth; for emotional magic, for invocations, for clearing, prophecy, initiations, love-magic, healing; for attuning with the very life-cycles of the world. It is also an excellent place for calling forth the undines and invoking the Goddess.

The mountaintop is the place for solar rituals; for attaining greatness in all things, for lifting yourself out of your life to look at it without prejudice; for seeking the truth, for success in the material life.

The cave is the place of feminine mysteries; it represents the womb and thusly the Goddess. It is a very sacred place and care must be taken that the emotions are not over-wrought while inside one. A sea cave or grotto is doubly powerful; here initiations were often performed. It is an excellent place for making requests of the Gnomes or, at the sea cave, one that has the ocean flowing in and out of it, of the Undines.

The blasted or lightning-struck tree is a place of masculine energy, and thus is perfect for banishing rituals of all types.

Standing stones, ancient earthworks, ruins, mounds, and all manner of prehistoric or very old sites are fine to work in if the magic and vibrations of the place are good and in harmony with you and all who work with you.

Stone circles can be excellent places too, but again, check to make sure there is no evil within.

To See Leys

Stand upon a tall hill or rock. Half-close your eyes, still your mind, and watch for faintly-glowing tracks cutting through the countryside. They will appear to cut straight through bushes, houses, or mountains. They will glow, either blue or greenish, or possibly yellow/goldish. The best time to do this is in the summer, at sunrise, or sunset, and best of all on Midsummer's Eve, just at sunset.

If others have seen these leys, they might have marked them with standing stones, buildings, roads, fences, hedges, and so on. But you may discover lines of energy never before known. Good luck!

Weather Predictions

Fair

Red sky at evening
Crescent Moon with horns upward
Owls hooting at night
Mist in the valley
Red lightning
Gnats sporting
Smoke rising straight up from the balefire
Clouds like wool
Evening rainbow
Bats coming out early in the evening
Birds coming out of their hiding places

Wind

Fiery sun at setting
Sharp horns on the sickle Moon
Sea surging; white-caps
Thunder in the morning
Leaves rustling in the forest
Spider webs in the air
Thistledown floating on the water
Herons flying above the clouds
Ducks flapping their wings

Rain

Yellow streaks in the sunset sky
Frogs croaking
Dark mist over the Moon
Twinkling stars
Red sky at morning
Leaves showing their backs
Crows agitating their wings
Birds flying away
Sheep frisking wantonly
Crickets chirping loudly

Storm

Shooting stars
Wolves howling
Sun pale at rising
Finches and sparrows chirping at dawn
Dry air
Birds fleeing from the sea
Bees not leaving their hives
Mice skipping around
Dogs rolling on the ground

Hard Winter Ahead

Trees holding their leaves
Tough apple skin
Early departure of birds
Bountiful crop of acorns
Large store of honey
Plants growing high

To See If the Rain Has Ended

If the rain has stopped, but you would know if for good, look to the sky. If you see birds, it is a good sign that it has stopped. However, to be sure, watch the birds in flight. Say aloud:

> Birds of the air
> Fly without care.
> Will it rain here?
> Will it rain there?

If they fly off, stop chanting and look closely to the direction they fly:

> To the East, 'twill be clear
> To the South, storm you'll hear
> To the West, never end
> To the North, Sun descend

Tapping Star Power

Sit out beneath the stars. It should be a clear night, but the warmer the better, since coolness makes it more difficult to tap the powers.

Bathe in the starlight; feel the brilliant white-bluish light flowing down onto your body. It is warm; it warms your muscles, relaxes you, and yet infuses you with a tremendous energy. Remember, the stars are suns, far away and yet affecting us and our world.

For visualization, see a star field in your mind. Pick out one star and propel yourself to it. Spread your hands out before you and take in as much energy through them as you can from the star. You do not have to approach the star too closely; when your hands start to burn you are close enough. To go on would be foolish. Stop and clutch the power within your hands. Come back down into your body and release the energy by flinging your hands, concentrating on your magical intent. So shall it be.

For communication, lie down on the earth on a cloudless or fairly clear night. In the mountains or desert, or far from the haunts of man, it is better, for the sky will be clearer for lack of nearby lights. Watch the stars overhead, picking out patterns at first, seeing how certain stars make pictures in the sky. Then diffuse your concentration; let go of your conscious mind; blank out all else but the stars. Open yourself to communication; see what the stars have to say to you.

The Tides and Ocean

Do positive, productive spells when the tide is coming in. Do destructive or banishing spells when the tide is going out.

High tide is the best time to do all spells; get a tide table and chart the highest tide around the date you wish to do your spell. If you can do the spell on the highest tide of the month, it is even better.

If you live near a large body of water your clairvoyant faculties will be stronger than if you live away from water.

Sea Shells

Sea shells are symbols of the Goddess and are excellent gifts. Wear them around the neck to honor her, or bless and pass to friends. They may also be used to symbolize the Goddess upon the altar, or even to contain salt or water upon the altar. They are used to draw money and prosperity, or to induce fertility.

With the large univalve shells, hold them up to the ear to induce a clairvoyant state. The sounds heard while doing this are called "the voice of the sea."

When doing rites on the seashore, you can mark out the Circle with shells.

The Holed Stone, or Witches Stone

On the seashore, find a stone with a hole in it; one that pierces the stone completely through. This is valuable in magic in many ways. Hang it up in the home as a protection, or around the neck. It can be placed upon the altar as a symbol of the goddess Diana, or put into water to bless and purify it. If you wish to see spirits, take the stone to a cemetery or wherever you believe spirits to be and look through the hole, keeping the other eye closed. This may also be used to facilitate astral vision in general, wherever you are. But this is best performed at night. This can also be tried to facilitate astral hearing, by placing the stone next to the ear. The Holed Stone is one of the most valuable of all Wiccan tools, and it is free, a gift of the Goddess.

The Four Basic Forms of Magic

The Image (poppets, roots, pictures, symbols, runes)
The Brew (potions, oils, simples and compounds, incense)
The Knot (cord magic)
The Charm (amulets and talismans, herbs, stones, symbols)

Take a black candle. Name it the person who is doing you harm, or rather, that person's power to do you harm. Now take it in both hands and break it. Then melt or bury it and things should look up. This won't hurt the person; only their effectiveness in harming you or the person you are working for.

Write what you want on a piece of paper, using a picture, runes, words, images, etc. Then place the appropriate herb in the center of the paper. Wrap this up in the paper, secure the ends, and throw into a very hot fire, stating or imaging your wish. So it will come to pass. This is called a "petition." Always thank the gods for what comes to pass.

The Magical Fluids of the Body

If you are right handed:

Your right hand is "electric" (masculine, commanding, vibrant, outward)

Your left hand is "magnetic" (feminine, passive, soothing, inward)

Use your right hand for directing power, for holding aloft your athame, or using it in place of your athame if it is not with you. Send energy *out* through your right hand; take energy *in* with your left.

If you are left handed, the above attributes should be reversed.

When you infuse an object with power, energy, or a special purpose, you have locked in the energy into that object. When this is done be sure to also set a release or key so that this energy can be released at any time, mentally. This is a great help when you are too sick or otherwise unable to raise this energy yourself. You can tap energy you have stored up in times of need. You needn't have the object with you; indeed the object need not be an actual object. But if you make it on the astral be sure you can image it exactly as you did when you locked energy into it.

Color Magic

Red Magic: matters of the body, both human and animal. This includes medicine, the military, hunting, physical strength, power, and zoology.

Orange Magic: matters of ego-strength, materialism, pride, self-confidence, courage, security.

Yellow Magic: mental faculties, mathematics, philosophy, learning, theorizing.

Green Magic: fertility, creativity, beauty, art, agriculture, herbalism.

Blue Magic: religion, ESP, spiritualism, psychic phenomena, social sciences, prophecy.

Indigo Magic: rain making and all weather working, astronomy, astrophysics, time travel, space exploration.

Purple Magic: love, lust, hate, fear, anger, ecstasy, politics.

Ultraviolet Magic: pure power.

Brown Magic: materialism, animals, ecology, hunting, the magic of woods and glens.

The above is a fairly modern method of categorizing magical methods by colors. Below is another, less organized, but highly effective system. Use the color indicated somehow in your ritual and it will be all that more effective. The powers of colors should not be underestimated.

Fertility	Green
Protection	White
Power	Purple, Red
Peace	White
Wealth	Green
Love	Green, Pink

Passion	Red
Pleasure	Green
Sex	Red
Honor	Gold
Travel	White, Yellow
Loss	Black
Death	Black
Change	Black
Life	Red
Health	Blue
War	Red
Conflicts	Red
Divination	Yellow
Success	Gold
Femininity	Green, Silver
Masculinity	Red, Gold
Courage	Red
Patience	Green
Creativity	Yellow
Optimism	Red
Compassion	Blue
Responsibility	Red
Confidence	Red
Tranquility	Green, Light Blue

Cord Magic

Take cord of the correct color for the intent involved and shape it on the altar or ground into a design of the thing you want: a car, money, peace, whatever. Send forth power and so shall it be.

Using the Tarot in Magic

There is a method of using the Tarot cards in magic; but it is one in which the card itself is consumed by the elements; therefore this can be costly, but a highly effective method.

The procedure begins with meditation on each of the seventy-eight cards. Sit quietly with the card, gazing at the symbols, and mentally invoke: For what would I use this card in magic? Record each card's magical use in a separate book. Do one card a night for seventy-eight nights. After this, buy several decks of the one you chose to do the meditations on.

Now, you are ready to use the Tarot. For this you must write your own rituals. For instance, if you were doing a spell to attract love, the Two of Cups might be appropriate. Since love is an attribute of Water, you might anoint the card with lotus oil, wrap it in blue silk, and toss it into the sea, imploring the Sylphs to grant you a love. Make up a chant to use along with the ritual.

Similarly all the cards can be used, in tune with the element, or planet, involved. If you were wishing to get rid of a bad habit, choose the card that most closely represents that habit and, after ritually naming it that habit, cut it up in pieces, burn the pieces, and bury the ashes. And so on with each type of ritual.

In this type of magic the card itself must be destroyed, or sent into an element, so that the power of the image is transferred to the rite. This is why you must have several decks available to use.

There is another type of Tarot magic in which the card is worn as an amulet or talisman. If a person seeks mastery over the elements, for instance, he or she might stitch a bag of a cloth that incorporates all four elemental colors into its design and put the Chariot card into this. This could then be anointed with the correct oils and carried while he or she is working on the elements.

Or if a person was having mental troubles, he or she might carry the Ace of Swords (or Wands, if he or she attributes that suit to the realm of Air, as many Wiccans do).

This system of magic is only sketchily presented here, because it is a very personal type. If you work with it, it can bring you excellent results.

A Healing

Bind the affected part of the body (i.e., the hand, arm, limb, torso, etc.) with red or black cord. Tie it tightly, saying the following:

> I *do not bind the* (name part of body). I *bind the disease residing there that it may leave the flesh and spirit of this person and enter the cord. Great Mother Cerridwen and Kernunnos, the Horned One, aid me in my work here. The disease is bound into the cord; only flames can release it hence! So mote it be!*

Untie the cord, touching it only as much as necessary. Throw it into a very hot fire. Visualize the disease melting, evaporating into the fire; it is being cleansed in the flames. This takes intense concentration, but works.

A Healing 2

Take a good strong magnet and stroke it over the afflicted spot several times while concentrating; the magnet absorbs the disease. Then bury the magnet for thirteen days off in the woods, away from living beings. Or, put a magnet in the bed and let it absorb the disease slowly. Or, wear a magnet. Always bury for thirteen days to release the sickness, then cleanse it and it can be used again, if it has not lost its power.

The Clover Spell

When you desire a wish to be granted:

Go to a hill on which the four-leaved clover grows. Pluck five of them by their stems and hold them up to the sky, saying:

> Lord *of the Day, Lady of Night, May you smile upon my rite.*

Then face north and, as you throw one clover in that direction, state your wish. Then repeat the procedure to the east, south, and west. When finished, face north again and eat the fifth clover. As it has become a part of you and your life, so too will your wish.

To Find a Lost Object

Still your mind. Stand in the room in which you believe you lost it. Then reach out your hand, without thinking of where you are reaching or in what direction. Chances are that will be the direction in which the object will lie.

To Change a Person's Mind

Look at the person's head. See it become clear, transparent. See the dust inside of it; the dust of his or her bad habits and ideas, the destructive ones. Dust it out with an astral feather duster (a red one, made of flame). It singes off all badness inside that person's mind—badness only, not the good. When you are done, remove the flame-duster and the head should go opaque again. It is done, but this is manipulation and should be used only with care.

Chant for Flying

Fly, Fly, Fly, thereby!
Up o'er the Mountains,
Up o'er the Seas!
Down in the Valleys,
Through the tall Trees!

Chant to produce astral projection.

To Be Said During the Dark of the Moon

Pray to the Moon when She be slivered
From ill you shall be delivered
What now harms you shall be bound
Down, down into the ground.

On a clean sheet of paper, write with a clean pen and lemon juice what you wish a person to do (sell you his home, be friendlier to you, etc.). Do this carefully. Let it dry. Now type or write your regular letter over this. Though they cannot see the invisible writing, their subconscious mind will read it and it will take effect. This works with cards, memos, letters, and so on. You could try using a stalk of a plant that had a good deal of sap in it to write with as well.

To Break a Spell Cast Upon You

Drink salt water.

Memory Reminders

Tie a knot in a yellow cord for each thing that must be remembered that day. Do this in the morning. Concentrate. See yourself remembering each thing as needed. Carry the cord with you and untie each knot as the thing is remembered.

Put one bead, pebble, or other small object in the pocket for each thing you wish to remember. Throw one out for each one as you remember it.

To Remove Obstacles, Bad Habits, Problems

Tie a knot in a black cord for each problem at the dark of the Moon, then burn it. Bury the ashes. As it goes up in flames, so too will your problems. It is best to work on one problem at a time; when that is solved, go on to the next one. This is what is meant by "power shared is power lost"; in other words, if you work on many projects your energy is divided; concentrate on one thing at a time and your magic will blossom.

Old Magical Tricks—The
Actual Magical Operations Involved

Listening to the Wind—clairvoyance

Flying—astral projection

Making Stones Speak—psychometry

Shape-Shifting—mind transference, illusion (when others see it)

Invisibility—astral projection

Water to Wine—illusion

Illusion magic was often used to scare away enemies, or to get one out
of a tight spot. It was never used for 'fun,' but always in earnest.

The Magic Mirror

Find a good, round mirror, of thirteen to thirty inches in diameter. Ideally, it should be encased in a similarly round frame, painted black, but
make do with what you can find.

After purchasing the mirror (without haggling over the price), bring
it home and wash the face carefully with a simple of mugwort. To make
a mugwort simple, steep one tablespoon mugwort in three cups hot
water for thirteen minutes; strain and cool before using.

When the mirror has dried, cover its face with a black cloth and lay
where it will not be touched until the Full Moon.

On that night, expose the mirror to the rays of the Moon, preferably
outside, but through a window if necessary. Charge the ritual mirror by
describing circles over it with your hands, palms down, the right hand
moving clockwise and the left counterclockwise, and saying:

Lady of the Moon, Great Diana,
You who sees all things and knows all knowledge,
I consecrate this mirror in your name,
That it might aid me in my magic.

Now, hang the mirror on an east-facing wall. Keep it covered when not
in use.

Expose the mirror to the rays of the Full Moon at least three times a year. When it gets dusty (if it should) wash with the mugwort simple.

If you wish, you may use a psychic oil to draw the symbol of the Moon on its back.

Some use the mirror as a means to achieve astral projection, but I don't recommend this. One can get the feeling that you are trapped in the mirror, and this can be dangerous to the newcomer.

Never use your mirror for anything other than magic. Have a separate mirror to use for everyday things: combing or brushing hair, and so on. Keep the magic mirror covered at all times when not in use.

Wiccan Mirror Lore

The first mirrors were lakes. The shiny blades of the Athames were also used as mirrors, and in place of the crystal, which is a mirror-like object as well.

All mirrors are symbols of the Moon and of the goddess Diana. If you would make a magic mirror, be sure that it is round.

The mirror is used in the admission rites for its sacred significance, much as it was used in the ancient Eleusinian Mysteries of Greece.

The mirror used by the Witches is always the silvered kind; the black type was used only by magicians, or by the Witches whom they protected during the Burning Times.

Sometimes it is good to have jewelry made with tiny mirrors on or in the piece; these are extremely protective. Polished silver jewelry can work well. Mirror jewelry "bounces back" evil and negativity; it should be washed every Full Moon in mugwort tea.

One form of protection against psychic attack is to visualize yourself wearing a coat of armor that is completely fashioned of mirrors; thus, no evil can reach you.

The Witch Balls of yesteryear were silvered globes, a combination of mirrors and crystal balls, and were hung in the windows or near the doors and chimney of the house to protect it and all its contents. Today these are hung on trees at Yuletide by people who have forgotten their original significance. Witch Balls are sometimes available and are well worth the price. Always keep them clean and shiny.

You can put a small, round mirror on the altar to symbolize the Goddess, if you cannot find a suitable statue.

A mirror may be hung up in the corner of the room to absorb negativity; or it can be hung on the south wall. See it as a vacuum onto the vastness of space; command all negativity, evil vibrations, influences, or entities to be sucked into it out of your room. Also put a block so that they cannot use the mirror as a doorway into this world. This is an excellent means to use in haunted houses, when the spirits simply will not go, or to exorcise a person. Seat them before the mirror and command the spirit to go into the mirror and into space.

Afterward, cleanse the mirror with vinegar, rubbing cut onions on the glass, or with your hands.

But never do this operation with your own magic mirror; it is permissible to use any other mirror you have, though.

Mirror Magic 1

Hang a small mirror in every corner of the attic (or highest point in the house) using red thread or cord, and say the following:

Mirror with the power to protect
I place thee so that thou may reflect
All evil to which this house may be subject!

Set twin white candles on both sides of the mirror, so that they will not be reflected. Sit or stand before it naked and say:

Oracle of Lunar Light,
Send me now the Second Sight.

Now gaze into the mirror, into your reflection's eyes. Gradually you will see another reflection; it will be that of a former life. It should be unmistakably familiar.

Stand before the mirror. Set twin candles of the appropriate colors on either side, then anoint the mirror's rim with the appropriate oil,

Next, with the oil, draw a circle upon the mirror, making sure the ends meet. Now stare into the center of the circle, where your eyes should meet those of your reflection. Concentrate, not on the scene, but on your wish. Then draw the rune corresponding to your wish on the mirror, with your Power hand. Cover the mirror until the next morning. It is done.

Mirror Magic 2

Stand before the mirror, by candlelight if possible. With lipstick or a grease pencil, or water soluble paint or ink, draw the runes of your desire onto the mirror. See them infused into your reflection, and know that such will be in your life. Then close your eyes and visualize your intent. It shall be done. Leave the markings on until the next morning, at which time you should wipe them off with a cloth, without looking at them.

Other Mirror-type Spells

The Sun and Glass Spell

Make an image or drawing of the evil influence or load a piece of paper with the thought. Direct the rays of the Sun with a mirror or through a burning-glass so that its power is concentrated upon the paper. As the paper burns, say:

> By Sun and Glass, and in the Gods' names,
> Thy power spent; thy form in flames,
> No more shall you bother me or mine;
> Begone! I charge you, in this sign.

To Divine with the Cauldron

On the night of the Full Moon, after the rites, take the cauldron to a place outside where you will not be disturbed. Bring also a coin of silver. Fill the cauldron with pure spring or lake water, then hold the coin up to the Moon, saying:

Lady of Light
Lady of Night
Strengthen the Sight
In this my rite.

Then draw the power of the Moon into the coin, using your visualization. Now, toss the coin into the cauldron. As it settles on the bottom, sit or kneel comfortably before it and gaze at the coin. If necessary, position the cauldron so that the Moon shines upon the coin. The sight will come. (Note: this works best with black cauldrons.)

The Sacred Lake

Lakes were once known as Diana's mirrors. On the night of the Full Moon, catch the reflection of the Moon on the still waters of a lake. Lie down and stare at the reflection, then blow gently on the water. The sight will come, if you pray to Diana to aid you.

To Improve the Appearance

Take a small round mirror, of about nine inches in diameter, dip it into the crystal clear water of a lake, stream, or spring, and say:

Clear as crystal,
Clear as air,
Make my form be
Fine and fair.

Then set up the mirror on the south wall at home. Every morning and evening stand before it and gaze into your reflection, concentrating on improving your appearance. So shall it be.

The Break-Glass Spell

Fill a box or bowl with broken glass. Press the flat side of your hand down upon it all at once, with equal pressure. You will not be hurt. As your hand is pressing against the glass, say:

Broken glass cannot hurt; All evil shall avert!

This is a protective spell to be used when you fear physical harm.

The Break-Mirror Spell

Set a small round mirror on the floor. Stand over it, holding a large rock. Do not stand so that you can see your image in the mirror, but look at the mirror's face and visualize your enemy, bad habit, problem, obstacle. Then drop the rock and watch the glass and your problem shatter into a million pieces.

Thus is the spell fixed.

To Destroy Another's Power to Do Harm

Make wax models of the aggressor's weapons (guns, tanks, swords, words, books, newspapers, etc.). Color and mold these to look as close to the actual objects themselves. When finished, sit before a fire (if possible) and take each model in your hands. Rub it slowly with your hands, warming it, disfiguring it. Say:

You are putty in my hands. You are powerless.

Repeat until you feel the time is right. Then throw the ruined model into the fire in the midst of the flames, saying:

You melt!

Visualize your enemy's power to do harm melting into the fire. Repeat for each object. This works also with a censer, if you make small wax models and have a fire going in it. The cauldron also serves to contain the fire for this spell.

On Finding an Amulet, Talisman, Charm, or Poppet

Do not touch. Scan. If it is evil, douse with rue oil, ignite, and with your palms held down over it, say:

Thy power spent, thy form in flames,
Be banished by the Great God's names!

Or whatever comes to mind. If you cannot burn it where it lies, move with wooden or glass or plastic utensils (not gloves) to a suitable place and perform the banishing. If rue or any other hex-breaking oil is not available, sprinkle with salt and burn. Bury or toss out ashes. Do not touch them!

Cacti are often used to send curses and hexes. Be wary. Scan any gift or object that is placed on your doorstep, desk and so on before you touch it. Protect, don't neglect!

The Knife and the Cauldron

Fill a cauldron (pot or bucket if you don't have a spare one) and place it just inside the door. Taking up a razor-sharp knife, place it point-down into the water, saying:

Into the water I place this blade
To guard against the thief and shade.
May no man or astral shell
Enter this place wherein I dwell.

This is an excellent protection spell, to be performed every evening before going to bed, or any time you feel the need.

Protective Stones

Take several small pebbles, of a different color than those on the ground surrounding your property, but not a hue that would stand out unduly. Take these pebbles, enough so that you have one for every square yard of your outdoor area, and put them on the floor before you. Hold your hands down over them and infuse them with protective qualities. Next, divide the pile into three parts. The middle part leave alone. The part on the left you will program to warn you of impending trespassers, to psychically tell you when someone is coming. The part on the right you will infuse with frightening visions of ghosts and ghouls and scary things, imaginary monsters, to frighten away those of weak minds and emotional instability. Thusly, you shall mix all the pebbles and scatter them across your property, but you must not be seen doing this. Thus placed, they shall do their work.

For Protection

Get a firm white or red onion, and a collection of black-headed pins, and take them before a fire or the altar. There, stick each pin into the onion, saying the following rhyme:

> I *pierce thee, I pierce thee,*
> *That thou may'st protect me.*

Continue to do this until the surface of the onion is completely covered with the pins. Place high in the room you spend the most time in, or in the attic, or up the chimney. This spell should be renewed every year, but the onion must not be touched while it is being taken down.

Protective Chant

Visualize a triple circle around your body and chant:

> I *am protected by thy might*
> O *Gracious Goddess, day and night.*

To Protect a Fireplace and Hearth

With white or red chalk, draw three circles directly before the fireplace on the hearth. This effectively guards the area. Renew every three months.

To Spell a Stone for Protection

When you have found a suitable stone, one which pleases your eye and finds favor in your hands, hold it tightly in your Power hand and say the following thrice:

> *Stone, evil you shall deny.*
> *Send it to the earth and sky.*
> *Send it to the flame and sea.*
> *Stone of power, protect me!*

The Circle of Stones Necklet

Make a necklet of twelve stones, of the same shape and size, and then put a thirteenth in of a different color and size, a larger one. Hold it up within the Circle of Stones and say:

> O *Circle of Stones, I ask that you infuse this amulet with your protection, a perfect pattern of protective energy, that it might protect my body, mind, and soul while I am outside the Circle of Stones. So said I,___, and So Mote It Be!*

This may also be used for wear within the Circle by altering the dedication slightly. If used out of the Circle, mark no signs or runes on it. However, if reserved for ritual use such can be painted or carved on.

```
THE CIRCLE OF STONES NECKLET

Make a necklet of twelve stones, of the same shape and size,
and then put a thirteen in of a different color and size, a larger
one.  Hold it up within the Circle of Stones and say:

    O Circle of Stones, I ask that you infuse this amulet
    with your protection, a perfect pattern of protective
    energy, that it might protect my body, mind and soul
    while I am outside the Circle of Stones.  So said I,
    _____, and So Mote It Be!
```

```
This may also be used for wear within the circle by altering
the dedication slightly.  If used for out-of-circle wear,
mark no signs or runes on it.  However, if reserved for ritual
use such can be painted or carved on.
```

To Be Said for Protection During a Lightning Storm

Mistress of the gentle rain
Master of the storm,
Guard against the ill and bane;
Shield me from harm.
And while fire flies through the air
And rain drops fiercely blast,
Keep my loved ones in your care
Til the storm is passed.

>*Wind, Wind, guard thy kin*
>*Flame, Flame do not maim*
>*Rain, Rain, leave amain*
>*Earth, Earth, guard my worth.*

The Candle Guardian

Place a lit candle in the window to guard your home while you are asleep. Be sure that it cannot tip over and that it will not crack the window glass or catch the curtains on fire; the offering or prayer candles in glass jars are perfect for this.

For Protecting a Person

To protect any person while they are away from you, throw a handful of sand, or grain, or rice after them as they leave, without their knowledge.

To Guard Your Food

3 needles
3 pins
3 nails

Put these into a jar of salt and keep in your cupboard to guard your food.

To Be Said for Protection While Walking Alone at Night

Hail Fair Moon,
Ruler of Night;
Keep me safe
Until the light!

Witches' Bottle

Pins, black-headed
Needles
Rosemary

Fill a bottle with the above. Add red wine to fill. Seal top with black wax. As you make your Witches' Bottle say the incantation, over and over, as you add each ingredient:

Pins and needles, rosemary, wine
In this Witches Bottle of mine
Guard from all harm and enmity:
This is my will, so mote it be!

This bottle should then be buried some distance from your home—off your property, preferably, but not too far. The bottle attracts negativity and ill-wishing away from you to itself.

Water Divination

Ask a yes/no question. Throw a pebble into a pool of water and count the rings which it forms. If the ripples are of an odd number, it means yes. If even, the answer is no.

Stone Divination

Find three stones, one dark, one light, and one of a unique color, different from the other two. Name one yes, one no, and use the strangely colored stone for the indicator. Ask a yes/no question. Shake the stones in your hands and throw them onto the ground or a table standing in the center of the room. The stone which is closest to the significator answers the question. Keep the stones in a pouch out of the sight of others when not in use, and let no one else touch them. (Note: if using a table and one of the stones falls off, there is no answer. Similarly, if the yes/no stones seem to be the same distance from the indicator stone, there is no answer. Try again later. Do no more than three throws a night.)

Bark Divination

Choose a broad and thin piece of bark. Put it into a bright fire and wait until it has caught. As soon as the flames have gone out, carefully remove it, without breaking it, and read the symbols made on the bark by the fire.

Flower Divination

Choose a flower at random, but do not pick it. Count the petals, saying yes or no until you reach the last. This answers your question. (Do not pluck the petals off, as non-witches do. There is no need to destroy nature; we work within and for it, not against Nature.)

Herb Incantation

Oh little plant of (name), *I ask that you give of your bounty that it may aid me in my work. Grow stronger by my stroke; stronger and more powerful, Oh little plant of* (name)!

Say this with love for the spirit of the plant. Take what you need, never more than 25 percent of the herb. Then place your offering (honey, an old coin, bread, an apple, red wine) at the base of the plant. If at all possible, never pick from the same herb twice during the lunar year.

Ancient Prayer to Herbs

"Now also I make intercession to you, all ye powers and herbs, and to your majesty: I beseech you, whom Earth the universal parent hath borne and given as a medicine of health to all peoples and hath put majesty upon, be ye now of the most benefit of humankind. This I pray and beseech you: be present here with your virtue, for she who created you hath herself undertaken that I may call you with the good will of him on whom the art of medicine was bestowed; therefore grant for health's sake good medicine, by grace of these powers aforesaid."

Used while preparing herbal mixtures for healing purposes. The "him" mentioned in this prayer was probably originally Aesculapius. This prayer is of Roman origin.

Wealth Sachet

Mix together cinquefoil, cinnamon, cloves, lemon balm, and a tonka bean or vanilla bean, whole. Do this on a Thursday after the Sun has set and while the Moon is in her increase. Sew up into a small purple or blue cloth bag and carry to increase riches.

Love Sachet

Take the petals of roses, well dried, a pinch of catnip, half a handful of yarrow, and a touch of mint, coltsfoot, strawberry leaves, orris root well-ground, tansy, and a bit of vervain. Mix well on a Friday evening in the Moon's increase, and divide into three parts. The first part throw up to the Moon while on bended knee, asking Diana that love be sent to you. The second part scatter around your bedchamber, and the third sew up into light green cloth. Wear this last upon your body, and love will surely appear.

Spell Balls

Take beeswax, warm it in your hand until it is soft and very flexible. Now take herbs of the correct type and mix these into the wax, all the while visualizing your intent. When the wax is well mixed with the herbs, form the wax imbedded with the herbs into balls, about an inch or so in diameter (they can be bigger, depending on your purpose, but it's easier to hide smaller balls).

Now lay the spell ball on your altar between two candles of the appropriate colors, depending on the sort of spell you're doing. Place your hands on either side of the spell ball and infuse it with energy, all the while visualizing.

Say the following incantation:

Cave, Mountain, Fire and Lake
All the Elements now wake
Charge this Spell Ball powerfully
This is my will, so mote it be!

If your intent is to gain money, put the spell balls wherever you might get money: in your desk at work, in your wallet or purse, in the mailbox; wherever. If it is a love-attracting spell, wear it close to your skin. Place where appropriate for your spell.

(Caution: spell balls can melt. Be careful! It's best to use these in the winter!) You can also string several spell balls into a necklace and wear this too.

Uses of Baneful Herbs by Witches

In the past, when the Wicca were the healers of the people as well as the priesthood and priesthood, many of the baneful herbs were used in practicing medicine. This knowledge was passed on by word of mouth, and was taught only the most eager and qualified pupil, by the most experienced herbal healer. These were the uses of these baneful herbs by the healers:

1. All healing aspects

2. Midwifery and abortions

3. Deadening pain (when removing arrowheads, etc.)

Herbs, especially the baneful kind, were also used as shortcuts to attain altered states of consciousness. They also came in handy when the magistrates and Witch-finders were about in the village or town. Here are these uses:

4. Inducing visions

5. Facilitating astral projection

6. Raising the power generally

7. Deadening pain during execution, especially during burning.

In light of this, an old Witch's tale should be told here. In Elizabethan times, Witches were taught that to be sure you would never be condemned to the scaffold (i.e., to be hanged), you should always carry a gilliflower with you. Gilliflower is another name for carnation. Why should this be? Perhaps because the carnation is an extremely powerful bloom; its scent is excellent for recuperating patients or those who have lost their will.

In the Burning Times, most of the Wicca were long gone from the towns and villages by the time the Witch-finders showed up, but the danger was always there. So it wouldn't surprise me at all to learn from a historical source that many suspected Witches in the 1600s wore gilliflowers, just in case!

Magical Baths

It's tradition to take a Magical Cleansing Bath at two times of the year:

Spring: Take a cleansing bath of marjoram and thyme.

Winter: Take a cleansing bath of bay, rosemary, and pine.

Of course, these are in addition to your regular cleansing baths.

Ritual Bath Salts

To one cup plain salt, add the appropriate oils until the scent seems right. The stronger the scent, the less salts will have to be used for each bath. Tint with food coloring.

Healing

Eucalyptus	13 drops	
Violet	7 drops	(tint greenish blue)
Carnation	13 drops	

Purification

Rose Geranium	13 drops	
Frankincense	7 drops	(leave white)
Rosemary	13 drops	

Circle (to be used when a bath sachet is not available)

Rosemary	3 drops	
Myrrh	3 drops	
Carnation	3 drops	(tint purple or leave white)
Lotus	3 drops	
Mint	1 drops	

Psychic (to be used before sleep for prophetic dreams)

Cassia	13 drops	
Anise	7 drops	(tint yellow)
Acacia	13 drops	

Magnetic (to be used prior to going out with the purpose of meeting people)

Women's Magnetic Bath:

Ambergris	3	
Gardenia	7	
Jasmine	9	(tint pink—love
Tuberose	7	blue—friendships
Violet	3	red—sexuality)

Men's Magnetic Bath:

Musk	3	
Patchouli	7	
Civet	9	(tint pink—love
Ambergris	7	blue—friendships
Cinnamon	3	red—sexuality)

Note: or add thirty drops of Venus oil [women] or Satyr oil [men]. Use this bath salt sparingly.

Druid's Fire

Ash logs
Elder logs
Vervain

Make a fire of these, using the vervain as the kindling. When it is burning well, add the following herbs:

Aster flowers
Meadowsweet
Mistletoe
Peppermint
Oak leaves
Betony

Use this fire for solar rituals.

The Old Dances and Music

Dancing was the first form of religious expression. It is not surprising, therefore, to learn that it was once a large part of Wiccan ritual.

In Traditionalist Wicca there were three main types of ritual dance: the Circle or Ring Dance, the Following Dance, and the Leaping Dance.

The Ring or Circle Dance began with the coven holding hands in the Circle, facing in. Sometimes in the center, on the altar (or on the ground if there was no altar) was a symbol, drawn on the ground, or an object, representing the thing that was desired (i.e., the reason the coven was working magic). This is known as the "object." The coven moved around the object with the intent of giving their wish power, and so through their physical effort the power was raised and sent through the group will of the coven.

This technique was also used for charging tools, jewelry, and so on.

An alternate type of Ring Dance had the coven leader standing in the center of the Circle, and when the power was raised to its maximum the leader told the coven to drop. The leader then sent forth the power.

If the dance was done for purely ritualistic purposes, it was usually accompanied by songs, sometimes calling upon the elements, or the gods, or just a simple seasonal song. These dances were always done deosil. Of course, if the Ring Dance was being done to banish a negative, it would be performed widdershins.

The Following Dance usually took place after the Ring Dance, if the former was done for ritual and not magic. The Circle broke off, the leader at the head. Releasing hands, the coven followed the leader across the countryside (or throughout the house, if it was a large one and the danger too great for outdoor activities). This was sometimes accompanied by all imitating animals, but this wasn't always the case. At its end, of course, the coven returned to the Circle, usually for the Feast. This type of dance usually occurred after the rituals, and was also used to train new Witches to move silently through the forest at night.

The Leaping Dance is really a variation on the Ring Dance. The coven, hands joined, leap over an object for various purposes. For instance, a stack of fruits and vegetables would be placed on the ground and all would leap over them to promote a good crop for the next harvest. Sometimes this was done with brooms, but this belongs to the feminine magic. It is said to be the origin of the Witch riding her broomstick.

The Leaping Dance was also done over sacred (small) stones, or cleansing fires. I also have a feeling that this might have been one of the old ordeals started during the Burning Times. The new Witch was laid down in the forest, alone, in the darkness, probably bound. Suddenly images passed over her; the coven ran and leapt over her. They continued this, one by one, for several minutes until the witch's fright and anxiety were gone. She had found trust in the coven, and was welcomed in.

Music was often used, especially before the Burning Times, to accompany the ritual and/or the dances. The music was traditionally made by a flute, a drum, and a harp of some kind, though often I feel just the drum was used for its ability to keep the coven moving as one through its beat. This beat was gradually increased in tempo while energy was raised, and set the emotional tone of the whole ritual.

The flute was always played by a man, for it was a symbol of the God; the drum by a woman, for it was a symbol of the Goddess; and the harp by a youth.

For more elaborate musical compositions, bells were added, though rarely after the Burning Times, as their voices could be heard through the night air clearly at a great distance.

A sistrum was sometimes also used in place of the bells, but this was only after the Cult of Isis reached Britain through the Romans.

Many of the old songs of the Craft have been lost; some are preserved in folk songs, such as "Greensleeves" and "Summer is A-Coming In." A study of folk music will reveal much. Most of the old Craft songs were in minor keys and fairly simple of tune and harmony and wording; but they were echoed throughout the land and were one of the main ways the Wicca had to preserve and pass on their lore.

Thus, the words or lyrics often contained stories of the gods, their deeds, and relations.

Today, unfortunately, most music is pre-recorded, though many covens are going back to the old ways.

A song we used to use around 1971 ran like this:

Diana and the Horned God
Will appear at Sabbat Time.
And lead us forth right pleasantly
To sup the Cakes and Wine;
To sup the Cakes and Wine my loves
And dance the magic round;
And lead us through the sacred rites
With joy and love unbound.

You will notice that the order of the ritual as described in this song is backward.

Originally, I'm sure, hand clapping or stomping of the feet or even banging on the cauldron was probably used as music. Drums were then invented to take care of that part.

In magical Wiccan symbolism the drum represents the element of Earth; the flute of Air; the lyre or harp of Fire; and the bell or sistrum of Water.

I have heard of rites wherein the athame is used to strike standing stones; this would produce tones of a sort, but was probably used for inducing clairvoyance or some other faculty, so this doesn't really fall under the heading of music.

The Story of the Sky People

In the time before time, in the vast reaches of the outer spaces, there existed a civilization on a planet much like Earth.

But this people were engaged in great civil war. In foreseeing their own destruction, the People of the Stars sent representatives of their race through space in silver needles, in search of new planets where their race might plant its seeds so that their knowledge and power would not be allowed to melt into the ground into nothingness.

One of the silver needles touched down upon the earth. The Sky People or Sky Lords mingled with Earth People, bred, and in so doing produced new priests and priestesses of the old powers. And from these people there arose the great technological/magical civilization known as Atlantis.

Mankind was taught the old secrets of tapping the forces of the universe; bending lines of energy; moving physical objects with their minds; seeing into the past, or future, or other's minds; healing the sick; calming wars and strife; as well as moving mountains, changing the courses of rivers, raising islands from the sea floor, activating volcanoes, and controlling the weather.

But for all their technological/magical achievements, the Atlanteans had a weakness—a weakness which those who had been the Sky People's adversaries were eager to capitalize on.

For the Sky People's enemies had followed the ships through space, determined to stamp out every trace of their very existence. So long as one outpost existed, these beings would not rest.

They came to Earth, found the work that the Atlanteans had accomplished, and knew that they could not bring about its destruction wholly by themselves, for they were few in number, the civil wars leaving few survivors and many dead on both sides.

Those beings plotted and influenced several of the key priestesses and priests in Atlantis. And in time this brought about its destruction.

But the blood of the Sky People lives on in our own; and the powers which they used lie in waiting to be tapped by those with the old knowledge.

And it is this power which is used in magic.

(Note: this is a legend and should be viewed as such.)

A Full Moon Ceremony

To a bath, add half cup of milk, three drops white wine, a bit of lemon rind to the water. Bathe and go to the rite.

Take sip of white wine. Close your eyes and meditate upon the Moon. See it rising above the horizon, travelling upward to rest directly above you. Bathe in the light; feel it cleansing and nurturing and strengthening you. Then get up, look at the real Moon and call your thanks to it. Light a white candle and let it burn while you are up that night. Eat grapes or mooncakes and white wine, melons or lettuce and lemonade. If there is a ring around the Moon, so much the better; her powers are tripled then.

Afterward, listen to soft music and meditate.

(Note: This ceremony should be used when you cannot attend a full meeting. It is also good to give to new students who cannot or should not attend the full rituals.)

Systems of Power

The elemental system was devised and refined in the Renaissance, but its roots stretch farther back into history. It can be viewed as nothing more than a convenient system of organization for the various types of magic. Then again, it may be viewed as a very real system of powers that can be called upon to aid spells and rituals. How you view the elements is up to you.

The following discussions deal with the symbolism of and types of magic related to the elements. All of the magic contained within this book falls under the rulership of one (or more) of the elements. This is true, too, of all that exists.

An understanding of the elements will aid your magical work immensely.

Though the elements are described as "masculine" or "feminine," this should not be viewed in a sexist way. This, like all magical systems, is symbolic—it describes the basic attributes of the elements in terms easily understandable. It doesn't mean that it is more masculine to perform Fire magic, or more appropriate for women to use Water magic. It's simply a system of symbols.

Excerpted from Earth Power *by Scott Cunningham*

THE ELEMENTS

The Elements

Earth

Gender: Feminine, passive

Color: Green

Time of Day: Midnight

Direction: North

Season: Winter

Tool: Pentacle

Point-in-life: Old Age

Tarot Suit: Pentacles

Qualities: Law, Understanding

Animals: Cow, Bison, Stag

Metal: Iron

King: Ghob

Spirits: Gnomes

Jewel: Rock Crystal, Salt

Places Ruled: Caves, Chasms, Fields, Groves

Natural Symbols: Acorn, Valleys, Caves, Rocks, Salt, Gravity

Musical Instruments: Drum, all Percussion Instruments

Astrological Signs: Taurus, Virgo, Capricorn

Magical Powers: Business, Money, Employment, Death, Binding Rituals, Food, Cooking, Agriculture

Sense: Touch

Positive Qualities: Growth, Solidarity, Foundation, Objectivity, Responsibility, Thoroughness, Practicality, Patience

Negative Qualities: Illusion, Dullness, Melancholy, Lack of Conscience, Boredom, Stagnation, Depression, Inflexibility

Type of Herb: Earthy, Dry and Stiff, Musty-Smelling, Roots, Heavy, Low-Growing, Mosses and Lichens, Ferns, Warm and Dry, Strong, Mellow-Scented, Nuts, Cave-Growing

Herbs of Earth

Patchouli	Ferns	Club Moss
Ambrette	Rice	High John the Conqueror
Parsley	Comfrey	Meadowsweet
Carnation	Woodruff	Pine
Dittany of Crete	Mandrake	Primrose
Storax	Oak	Nuts
Thrift	Valerian	Ivy
Oats	Lady's Slipper	Barley
Cypress	Wood Betony	Wheat
Cedar	Horehound	Corn

Earth is the *base* of the Witch; it is this sphere in which we operate the most. Earth is also the realm of fertility and so this power is invoked to cause fruition of all magical operations.

Earth is the element of silent abundance, of foundation. It is physical, but should be lauded because it supports all the other elements; without Earth, life as we know it would not exist.

Magic of this realm is of the fruits: herbs, flowers, trees, and all growing things. The ancient gods and goddesses of the Earth—Demeter, Mah, Persephone, Kore, Ceres, Marduk, Gaea, Rhea, Dagda, Silvanus, Pan, and Osiris, among many others, represent the continuing life-force of the element of Earth.

Earth is the womb of the Goddess and the ancients buried their dead within her, laying them in a fetal position and dusting them with red powders representing the blood of renewed life. As we proceed from the Goddess, so we must return to her, on the Wheel of Reincarnation and through the Earth.

Offerings and invocations to the Earth realm should be buried.

Air

Gender: Masculine, Active

Color: Yellow

Time of Day: Dawn

Direction: East

Season: Spring

Tool: Wand, Censer

Point-in-life: Childhood

Tarot Suit: Swords

Qualities: Life, Faith

Animals: Eagle, Hawk, All Birds

Metals: Copper, Tin

King: Paralda

Spirits: Sylphs

Jewel: Topaz

Places Ruled: High Mountain Tops, Wind-swept Hills, Plains, High Towers

Natural Symbols: Feather, Birds, Wind, Clouds, Smoke

Musical Instruments: Flute, all Wind Instruments

Astrological Signs: Gemini, Libra, Aquarius

Magical Powers: Disputations, Moving, Travel, Weather Working, Instruction, Freedom, Knowledge, Gossip, Theory

Sense: Hearing/Smell

Positive Qualities: Freedom, Diligence, Dexterity, Optimism, Joy of Living, Intelligence

Negative Qualities: Contempt, Slyness, Gossiping, Lying, Diffidence

Type of Herb: Airy, Intellectual, Mental, borne by the Air, Flowers, heavily scented

Herbs of Air

Spearmint	Mint
Mistletoe	Lemon Balm
Lavender	Orange Flowers
Hazel	Mugwort
Cherry	Pimpernel
Aspen	Sandalwood
Mastic	Slippery Elm
Benzoin	Solomon's Seal
Eyebright	Star Anise
Rose	Wormwood
Catnip	Yarrow

Air is the *mind*, the *intellect* of the Witch. It is the element of movement, of freshness. Magic of this realm is mental or inertia-creating. It is used to "get something off the ground."

Gods and goddesses of the Air include Hera, Shu, Arianrhod, Nuit, Enlil, Mercury, Thoth. Offerings to this element should be thrown into the air.

Fire

Gender: Masculine, Active

Color: Red

Time of Day: Noon

Direction: South

Season: Summer

Tool: Sword/Athame

Point-in-life: Youth

Tarot Suit: Wands

Qualities: Light, Hope

Animals: Lion, Dragon

Metals: Gold, Iron

King: Djinn

Spirits: Salamanders

Jewel: Fire Opal

Places Ruled: Deserts, Volcanoes, Hot Springs

Natural Symbols: Flame, Lightning, the Sun

Musical Instruments: Lyre, all Stringed Instruments

Astrological Signs: Aries, Leo, Sagittarius

Magical Powers: Energy, Power, Authority, Prestige, Domination, Compulsion, Sex, Passion, Healing, Change, Destruction, Evolution, Purification, Heat, all Men

Sense: Sight

Positive Qualities: Courage, Daring, Enthusiasm, Valor, Patriotism Against Evil, Energetic, Assertiveness, Dedication

Negative Qualities: Anger, Jealousy, Bitterness, Spite, Vindictiveness, Hatred, Sex Obsession, Impatience, Smoking, Pyromancy

Type of Herb: Fiery, Biting, Stinging, Growth-Inhibiting, Warm, Stimulating, Angry or Passionate, Sun Symbols, Seeds, Spiny, Spokey, Bitter, Spicy

Herbs of Fire

Dragon's Blood	Holly	Sunflower
Red Sandalwood	Cinnamon	Marigold
Saffron	Cassia	Mullein
Mustard	Dill	Myrtle
Garlic	Red Anemone	Nutmeg
Pepper	Heliotrope	Onion
Nettle	Southernwood	Periwinkle
Thistle	Basil	Snapdragon
Rue	Bay Laurel	St. John's Wort
Sorrel	Celandine	Thyme
Frankincense	Coriander	Vervain
Red Geranium	All Cacti	Violet
Red Poppy	Cloves	Hyssop
Vanilla	Curry Leaf	Tobacco
Mandrake	Hibiscus	

Fire is the *will* of the Witch. It is invoked to cause *change*, usually through destruction of what is, to bring forth that which can be. Water cleanses; Fire purifies.

It is also the realm of sexuality, and passions of every nature.

Fire is the one element always present on the Witch's altar, for it symbolizes the "spark of life" that resides within all humanity.

We should be wary of Fire; its touch burns, and by it we learn. Change never occurs without a death, however great or small it may be. The past must die to make way for the future.

The Fire-nature of man is the most seen—anger, spite, hostility, and in such good manifestations as industriousness, will to live, action. Unfortunately, Fire blinds us, so that these qualities take precedence, and action is accomplished without intellect; destruction without compassion; hatred without foundation.

Fire quickly spreads, but only as long as fuel exists. It must be first tempered with *Water*, to cool its flames, and be fed *Air*, to show the error of its ways.

The Sacred Fire, or sexual passion, is a gift residing within. All should enjoy and use this gift. However, when the Fire flares up into an inferno and runs a person's life, there is an imbalance and action must be taken.

Fire can have one of the strongest influences of the elements, and its scars last, but the flames can be quickly killed by immersing yourself in Water consciousness.

The Fire gods and goddesses include Vesta, Hestia, Vulcan, Pele, Brigit, and Horus.

Offerings to Fire should be burned in a very hot fire.

Water

Gender: Feminine, Passive

Color: Blue

Time of Day: Dusk, Sunset

Direction: West

Season: Autumn

Tool: Chalice/Cauldron

Point-in-life: Maturity

Tarot Suit: Cups

Qualities: Love, Charity

Animals: Dolphins, Fish, Seals, all Sea Creatures

Metal: Mercury (Quicksilver)

King: Nicksa

Spirits: Undines

Jewel: Aquamarine

Places Ruled: Pools, Springs, Wells, Lakes, the Sea, Beaches

Natural Symbols: Lakes, the Ocean, Rain, Fog, Mist, a Wave

Musical Instruments: Sistrum, Cymbal, Gong, any Resonant Metal

Astrological Signs: Cancer, Scorpio, Pisces

Magical Powers: Pleasure, Marriage, Handfastings, Fertility, Happiness, Gatherings, Sex, Love, Sleep, Prophetic Dreaming, Learning and Absorbing

Sense: Taste

Positive Qualities: Compassion, Tenderness, Receptivity, Forgiveness, Fluidity

Negative Qualities: Close-mindedness, Instability, Indifference, Spine-lessness, Uncomittedness, Rudeness, Negligence

Type of Herb: Fleshy, Watery, Grows On, Near, or In Water, are Loving, Emotional, Dreamy, Drowsy, and Leafy Plants

Herbs of Water

Grapes	Lettuce	Camphor
Jasmine	Lotus	Cucumber
Kelp and Seaweeds	Henbane	Sugar Beets
Loosestrife	Camomile	Lovage
Poppy	Deadly Nightshade	Hemp
Orange	Willow	Lemon
Watercress	Melons	Hops
Orris Root	Scullcap	Pansy
Tonka Bean	Tormentil	

Water is the *love* of the Witch. It is the *emotional* base by which everything is influenced. It is the emotional element due to the fluid nature of our emotions. But fluidity can be both virtue and vice; Water should not be left untended or unexamined.

Water is the element of love, of absorption, of fertility. It is traditionally thought of as feminine, as Fire is masculine. The subconscious is symbolized by this element; rolling, always moving, germinating, like the sea which rests not day or night. The conscious mind is symbolized by Air.

The great flood so fabled today was a manifestation of the cleansing power of Water. Thus, Water is symbolic of purity, and is employed in baptismal rites the world over.

Water is cool, but never cold; comforting and gently moving. It is all around us; rain is cleansing, not only to physical objects, but also to the vibrations raised in those places inhabited by humans.

Bathing is a meeting of Water and mankind; it should be slow, drowsing, and dreamy. Never force Water to cause something to happen; it must be gently persuaded, and once you have dropped a wish into the pool of Water it will send out its rings and will come to fruition if the tides and streams be just and good. And if the wish be just and good.

The gods of Water and the Seas include: Eura, Nea, Fontus, Dylan, Poseidon, Amphitrite, Feronia, Varuna. There are also innumerable Well, River, and Lake gods and goddesses; mythology is full of them.

The Planets

The Sun

Masculine, Regal, Hot, Dry, Positive

Vocations: Theatre, Film, TV, Radio, Film Producers, Politicians, Executives, Financiers, Directors, Diplomats, Superiors, Officials, all Employers, Heads of Groups

Gods of the Sun: Apollo, Adonis, Ra, Baal, Balder, Helios, Horus, Mithras, Arthur, Herne

Music: "Firebird Suite" (Stravinsky), "The Great Gate" (Kiev)

Keywords: Vitality, Individuality, Will, Power, Leadership, Vigor, Ego, Masculine Principle, Creativeness, Authority

Jewels and Metals: Gold, Carbuncle, Diamond, Chrysolite, Topaz, Citrine

Animals and Birds: Lion, Eagle, Cock, Ibis, Parrot, Horse, Swan, Sparrow-Hawk, Phoenix, Dragon

Numerical Value: 6

Colors: Gold, Orange

Symbols: Flashes of Light, Lightning, Sparks, Fire, Naturally Light-emitting Objects, Warmth

Day of Week: Sunday

Perfume and Scents: Cinnamon, Myrrh

Places Ruled: Palaces, Mountains, Meadows, Sunshine, Groves, Upper Rooms

Wood: Oak or Laurel

Herbs: The Sun rules all gums, such as frankincense, mastic, benzoin, storax, and laudanum. Of herbs, it has dominion over those which display a golden color (saffron), or a like shape (sunflower), or a habit of turning toward the sun, as the heliotrope. It also rules many plants which bear gold or orange-colored blossoms.

Angelica	Heliotrope	Saffron	Frankincense
Peony	Lovage	St. John's Wort	Mastic
Ash	Marigold	Storax	Benzoin
Bay	Corn	Sundew	Myrrh

Burnet	Rice	Sunflower	Arnica
Camomile	Mistletoe	Tormentil	Damiana
Celandine	Laudanum	Vine	Henna
Centaury	Rosemary	Pineapple	Orange
Eyebright	Rue	Grapefruit	Cashew
Cassia	Heart Trefoil	Olive	
Cinnamon	Walnut	Holly	
Ginseng	Almond	Cloves	
Juniper	Coconut	Raisins	
Oak	Helianthus	Peanut	

Beverages: Red Wines, Coffee, Tea, Orange Juice, Grapefruit Juice, Mead

Tone: D

Body-Wise: Spleen, Heart, Spine, Right Eye, Front Pituitary Gland, part of the Thyroid, Vital Fluid, Oxygen

Types of Spells: Healing, Divine Power, Labor, World Leaders, all operations involving Employers and Promotions and Politicians

The Moon

Feminine, Cold, Moist, Negative

Vocations: Housekeeping, Cooking, Washing, Animal Husbandry, Sailing, Naval Services, Fishing, Hotels, Real Estate, Inns, Food Industry, Clairvoyant (Professional)

Goddesses of the Moon: Hecate, Diana, Isis, Lucina, Selene, Artemis, Luna, Cynthia, Phoebe, Anna, Hathor

Music: "Clair de Lune" (Maiden aspect), "Hymn to the Moon" from *Turandot* (The Crone) and the "Hymn to the Sun" from the opera *Le Coq d'Or* (The Great Mother)

Keywords: Domestic, Instinctual, Impressionable, Nourishing, Receptivity, Feminine Principle, Fecundation, Response, Fluctuation, Mirror Image

Jewels and Metals: Moonstone, Pearl, Silver, Emerald, Beryl, Crystal, Quartz

Animals and Birds: Shellfish, Mosquito, Bat, Moth, Rabbit, Hare, Nightingale, Snail, Frog, Cat, Swan, Owl, Field-Mouse, Elephant, Goose, Doe, Otter

Numerical Value: 9

Colors: White, Silver, Light Green

Symbols: Mirrors, Crystal Balls, Lakes, Round Seashells, Milk

Day of Week: Monday

Perfume and Scents: Camphor, Jasmine, Sandalwood

Places Ruled: Wildernesses, Woods, Rocks, Forests, Lakes

Wood: Willow

Herbs: The Moon rules the leaves of herbs such as have a cold nature, such as the lettuce, and the wintergreen. Herbs of other kinds it rules are those with soft, juicy leaves, those that live in or near water, nocturnal plants, those with large, watery fruits, and those that show a lunar signature, such as honesty, the moonwort, and the senna.

Acanthus	Lily	Saxifrage
Yellow Flag	Camphor	Adder's Tongue

Moonwort

Eucalyptus

Water Lily

Cucumber

Melons

Pumpkin

Lotus

Wintergreen

Lettuce

Banana

Sweet Sedge

Night-Blooming Cereus

Endive

All Gourds

Wallflower

Chickweed

Cabbage

Privet

Wild Rose

Willow

Iris

Breadfruit

Purslane

Sugarcane

Clary Sage

Rhubarb

Some Mushrooms

Lemon

Lemon

Poppy

Golden Seal

Watercress

Dwarf Rocket Grass

Mango

Turnip

Seaweeds

Senna

Kiwi Fruit

Arrach

Ardue

Sea Holly

Beverages: Lemonade, White Wine, Milk, Cream

Tone: F

Body-Wise: Esophagus, Uterus, Ovaries, Left Eye, Breast, Lymph System, Nervous System, Thymus Gland

Types of Spells: Clairvoyance, Dream-Working, the Sea, Cooking, Agriculture, Fertility, Medicine, the Home and Family

Mercury

Hermaphroditic

Vocations: Publishing World, Editors, Writers, Librarians, Booksellers, Communications Companies, Professors, Teachers, Aircraft Industry, Philosophers, Salesmen

Gods and Goddesses of Mercury: Thoth, Hermes, Anubis, Athena, Maat

Music: "Classical Symphony" (Prokofiev) or "Mercury" (Holst, *The Planets*)

Keywords: Intellectualism, Creativity, Science, Eloquence

Jewels and Metals: Carnelian, Aquamarine, Agate, Mercury (Quicksilver), Aluminum, Alloys of all sorts, Electrum (Alloy gold and silver), Orange Topaz, Quartz, Opal

Animals and Birds: Fox, Monkey, Lynx, Spider, Ant, Weasel, Laughing Hyena, Swallow, Magpie, Ibis, Ape, Stork, Snake

Numerical Value: 8

Color: Yellow

Symbol: Wings

Day of Week: Wednesday

Perfume and Scents: Mace, Narcissus

Places Ruled: Public Places, Cities, Places of Learning

Wood: Hazel

Herbs: Mercury rules all peels and parings of wood and fruit, such as mace, citron peel, laurel berries, and all odoriferous seeds. Of herbs those which have a fine and airy nature; those with finely divided leaves and stems, such as grasses, and ferns; those that have a subtle odor; and those that are important as food.

Calamint	Dill	Caraway
Elecampane	Fennel	Fenugreek
Flax	Hazel	Horehound
Lavender	Lily of the Valley	Licorice
Maidenhair	Marjoram	Mulberry
Mushroom	Myrtle	Pomegranate
Savory	Smallage	Southernwood

Starwort	Trefoil	Valerian
Mace	Citron	Bay Laurel
Celery	Carrot	Oats
All Ferns	All Grasses	Nutmeg
Parsley	Parsnip	Brazil Nut
Spurge	Horsetail	Hound's Tongue
Cascara	Sagrada	

Beverages: Pomegranate Juice, Carrot Juice, Celery Juice

Tone: B

Body-Wise: Brain and Nervous System, Thyroid, Respiratory and Pulmonary Circulation, Nerve Impulses, Mouth, Tongue, Parathyroid Gland, Right Cerebral Hemisphere, Auditory Nerves, Vocal Cords

Types of Spells: Studying, Teaching, Divination, Predictions, Self-Improvement, Communications of Every Kind, the Mind, Celibacy

Venus

Feminine, Benefic, Warm, Moist, Fruitful, Negative/Lesser in Fortune

Vocations: Art and all Artists, Musicians, High-Fashion Models, Perfumists, Hair Dressers, Manicurists, Singers, Painters, Interior Decorators

Gods and Goddesses: Aphrodite, Hathor, Venus, Astarte, Freya, Ishtar, Eros, Pan, Mari

Music: "Venus" (Holst, *The Planets*), "Violin Concerto #1" (Max Bruch)

Keywords: Luxury, Beauty, Love, Pleasure, Celebration, Sex, Partnerships, Harmony

Jewels and Metals: Copper, Emerald, Turquoise

Animals and Birds: Butterfly, Bee, Partridge, Peacock, Sheep, Goat, Lynx, Camel, Dove

Numerical Value: 7

Color: Green

Symbol: Beautiful Woman, comb and mirror

Day of the Week: Friday

Perfume and Scents: Ambergris, Musk, Benzoin, all expensive Perfumes and Essential Oils, Attar of Rose, Jasmine

Places Ruled: Fountains, Meadows, Gardens, Seashores, Beauty Parlors

Wood: Apple or Myrtle

Herbs: Venus has dominion over all sweet flowers, such as roses, violets, and the like. Also those herbs with showy flowers, a pleasant smell, and those with smooth, green foliage and fruits, sometimes with a blush or red, as the apple, or green flowers.

Apple	Alder	Birch
Blackberry	Burdock	Catnip
Cherry	Coltsfoot	Columbine
Daffodil	Daisy	Dittany of Crete
Wheat	Feverfew	Beans
Strawberry	Foxglove	Tansy
Peas	Thyme	Lentils
Vervain	Geranium	Violet

Goldenrod	Woodsage	Mallow
Yarrow	Mint	Peach
Mugwort	Primrose	Pennyroyal
Alkanet	Periwinkle	Rose
Fleabane	Groundsel	Melilot
Plantain	Tomato	Gooseberry
Witch Hazel	Lemon Verbena	Spearmint
Artichoke	Apricot	Fig
Plum	Grape	Peach
Raspberry	Blackberry	Olive
Elder		

Beverages: Cherry Juice, Cherry Wine, Tomato Juice, Apricot Nectar, Plum Wine, Grape Juice, Apple Cider, Mint Julep

Tone: E

Body-Wise: Venous Blood, Veins, Skin, Hair, Sense of Touch, Throat, Cheeks, Kidneys

Types of Spells: Love, Pleasure, Art, Music, Incense and Perfume Composition, Partnerships, Rituals Involving Women, Friendships, Herbalism

Mars

Masculine, Malefic, Hot, Dry, Positive/Lesser in Fortune, Barren

Vocations: Armed Services, Engineering, Dentistry, Chemistry, Barbers, Surgeons, Butchers and Meat Processors, Police, Carpenters, Sheriffs. All War-related vocations. Herd production, Sports (especially violent ones), Hunting.

Gods and Goddesses: Ares, Minerva, Mars, Hu, Horus, Athena, Bellona

Music: All Marches, "Mars" (Holst, *The Planets*)

Keywords: Aggression, Passion, Energy, Surgery, Blood, Mindlessness, Vengeance

Jewels and Metals: Bloodstone, Garnet, Ruby, Jasper and Iron

Animals and Birds: Scorpions, Venomous Snakes, Wasp, Hornet, Hawk, Vulture, Hyena, Tiger, Wolf, Mule, Donkey

Numerical Value: 5

Color: Red

Symbols: Blood, Drawn Sword, Gun

Day of Week: Tuesday

Perfume and Scents: Benzoin, Sulphur, Tobacco

Places Ruled: Battlefields, Bakehouses, Glass houses, Shambles, Places of Execution, Police Stations, Prisons

Wood: Hawthorn

Herbs: Mars rules herbs that possess thorns, spines, or prickles (save the rose), such as the hawthorn, thistle, brambles; those that live in dry places and deserts, such as cacti; those that have stimulating properties such as pepper, or onion; and those that show a red color.

Anemone	Barberry	Basil
Briony	Broom	Galangal
Garlic	Hawthorn	Honeysuckle
Hops	Wormwood	Onion
Parsley	Pepper	Radish
Pimento	Rhubarb	Rocket
Sarsaparilla	Tarragon	Tobacco
Woodruff	Thistles	Coriander

Cascarilla	Ginger	Chives
Lesser Celandine	Wild Lettuce	Tamarind
Pitcher Plant	Cloves	Bramble
Madder	Gorse	All Cacti

Beverages: Ginger Ale, Root Beer, Tequila

Tone: C

Body-Wise: Muscular System, Red Corpuscles, Gonads, Adrenalin, Motor Nerves

Types of Spells: Lust, Physical Strength, Courage, Politics, Debates, War, Contests, Competitions, Men, Conflicts, Hunting, Surgery, Athletics

Jupiter

Masculine, Benefic, Warm, Fruitful, Positive

Vocations: Money Handling, Bank Teller, Government, Politicians, Church, Explorers, Discoverers, Officials, Advertising, Credit-Collection and Savings Institutions, Gambling, Speculating, Stock Market

Gods and Goddesses: Jupiter, Zeus, Cronos, Osiris, Hera, Juno, Themis, Marduk

Music: "Jupiter" (Holst, *The Planets*), "March of the Meistersingers" (Wagner), "New World Symphony" (Dvorak)

Keywords: Expansion, Purging, Generosity, Growth, Wealth

Jewels and Metals: Amethyst, Tin, Turquoise, Lapis-Lazuli, Dark Sapphire

Animals and Birds: Hart, Eagle, Unicorn

Numerical Value: 4

Color: Purple or very dark Blue

Symbol: Coin of the Realm (dollar bill, pennies)

Day of the Week: Thursday

Perfume and Scents: Balm, Cinnamon, Nutmeg

Places Ruled: Theatres, Music Houses, Banks, Vaults

Wood: Fir or Pine

Herbs: Jupiter rules odoriferous fruits, such as the clove, nutmeg, etc. Also the herbs often show the pattern of four, to honor Jupiter's number. The plants are often large, edible, nutritious, and have a pleasant odor; those with purple or violet flowers.

Agrimony	Endive	Hollyhock	Asparagus
Hyssop	Vanilla Bean	Avens	Jasmine
Salsify	Balm	Myrrh	Chestnut
Betony	Oak	Papaya	Borage
Pinks	Meadowsweet	Chervil	Sage
Viper's Bugloss	Cinquefoil	Sumac	Bilbury
Costmary	Datura	Anise	Dandelion
Turnip	Toadflax	Dock	Nutmeg
Currants	Tonka Bean		

Beverages: Papaya Nectar, Dandelion Wine, Jasmine Tea

Tone: A

Body-Wise: Arterial System, Liver, Fats, Pancreas Secretions (Insulin), Adrenals

Types of Spells: Wealth, Prosperity, Monetary Matters, Legal Matters, Luck, Materialism, Expansion

Saturn

Feminine, Malefic, Cold, Dry, Barren, Negative

Vocations: Landlords, Landowners, Antique Sales, Real Estate, Steel Construction Workers, Concrete Manufacturers, Stone Masons, Research Scientists, Farm Workers, Retirement Homes/Workers, Undertaking Services and Mortuaries, Graveyards and Grave Diggers, Historic Buildings, Excavations, Archaeologists, Museum Workers.

Gods and Goddesses: Isis, Demeter, Marah, Kali, Kronos, Saturn, Ninib, Hecate

Music: Funeral Marches, Dirges, "Saturn" (Holst, *The Planets*). Shostakovitch's "Symphony #1"

Keywords: Death, Decay, Separation, Buildings, Fate, Ancient, Time

Jewels and Metals: Chalcedony, Onyz, Black Coral, Jade, Jet, Sardonyx, Malachite, Lead

Animals and Birds: Vulture, Beetle, Crustaceans, Mole, Owl, Beaver, Pig, Bear, Goat, Crane, Ostrich, Crocodile, Lapwing, Dragon, Crow

Numerical Value: 3

Color: Black

Symbol: Dust

Day of Week: Saturday

Perfume and Scents: Civet, Alum, Musk

Places Ruled: Vaults, Tombs, Monasteries, Catacombs, Empty Buildings, Caves, Dens, Pits

Wood: Poplar or Alder

Herbs: Saturn rules roots such as the pepper-wort root, and in herbs rules those with insignificant flowers, dull green foliage, unpleasant taste and smell, and nearly every baneful herb, such as the hellebore, the nightshades, and plants with black or very dark flowers.

Aconite	Hellebore	Mullein
Yew	Barley	Hemlock
Nightshade	Woad	Beet
Henbane	Poplar	Spinach
Comfrey	Hemp	Ragwort

Bistort	Cypress	Holly
Sloe	Quince	Potato
Ivy	Tamarisk	Solomon's Seal
Elm	Juniper	Thrift
Asafoetida	Fumitory	Knotgrass
Willow	Bistort	Cress
Mosses of all kinds	Houseleek	Mandrake
Nux Vomica	Horsetail	Dodder
Cocklebur		

Beverages: Vodka

Tone: G

Body-Wise: Spleen, Bones, Ligaments, Teeth, Mineral Salts, Inner Ear, Gall Bladder, Skin, Bones

Types of Spells: Buildings, the Elderly, Funerals, Wills, Destroying Diseases and Pests, Breaking Bad Habits, Terminations of all kinds

Astrological Color Correspondences

The following are lists of color correspondences. These should be consulted when devising your own rituals.

Aries	Scarlet Red
Taurus	Blue
Gemini	Yellow
Cancer	White, Green, Silver
Leo	Gold, Yellow
Virgo	Blue, Violet, Yellow
Libra	Lavender, Blue
Scorpio	Red, Russet, Brown
Sagittarius	Orange, Purple
Capricorn	Indigo
Aquarius	Blue, Green
Pisces	Purple, Green

The Moon

New Moon: White, symbolizes the Maiden
Full Moon: Red, symbolizes the Mother
Old Moon: Black, symbolizes the Crone

The Elements

Air   Yellow
Fire   Red
Water   Blue
Earth   Green

The Planets

Sun   Gold, Yellow
Moon   Silver, White
Jupiter   Blue, Purple
Mars   Red
Mercury   Yellow
Venus   Green
Saturn   Black

The Seasons

Winter is the WHITE of snow
Spring is the GREEN of plants
Summer is the GOLD of the Sun
Fall is the RED of the falling leaves

Days of the Week

Sunday   Gold or Orange
Monday   Silver or White
Tuesday   Red
Wednesday   Yellow
Thursday   Purple
Friday   Green
Saturday   Indigo or Black

Robe Colors as Used in Some Covens

Brown: Those who work with animals

Green: Those who work with herbs

Blue: Those that heal

White: Those that write poetry and song and musicians

Purple: Those who work with Power (i.e., magicians)

Yellow: Those who see (i.e., clairvoyants)

Gold: High Priest

Silver: High Priestess

Candle Colors

White:	Purity, Truth, Peace, Sincerity
Red:	Strength, Health, Vigor, Sex
Black:	Discord, Confusion, Banishment, all that is bane
Light Blue:	Tranquility, Understanding, Patience, Healing
Dark Blue:	Impulsiveness, Depression, Changeability
Green:	Finance, Fertility, Luck
Silver/Gray:	Cancellation, Neutrality, Stalemate
Gold/Yellow:	Attraction, Persuasion, Charm, Confidence
Brown:	Hesitation, Uncertainty, Neutrality
Pink:	Honor, Love, Morality
Orange:	Encouragement, Adaptability, Stimulation, Attraction
Light Green:	Sickness, Cowardice, Jealousy, Discord

Cord Colors

Red: Body (Physical)—First Level

White: Mind (Mental)—Second Level

Blue: Soul (Spiritual)—Third Level

The Body and Astrology

Aries: Head

Taurus: Neck

Gemini: Shoulders and Lungs

Cancer: Stomach and Breast

Leo: Heart and Back

Virgo: Intestines

Libra: Loins and Kidneys

Scorpio: Genitals

Sagittarius: Hips and Thighs

Capricorn: Knees

Aquarius: Legs and Ankles

Pisces: Feet

The Body and the Elements

Earth: Feet, Legs, Bowels

Water: Abdomen

Air: Chest

Fire: Shoulders, Neck, Head

The Numbers

Even numbers are masculine, odd are feminine:

1 is the number of life, of the Universe, of Dryghtyn.

2 is the perfect duality; polarity, male/female couple.

3 is the Triple Goddess; the lunar phases; the physical, mental, and spiritual bodies of human kind.

4 is the elements, Spirits of the Stones, the quarters, winds, and so forth.

5 is the senses, the pentagram.

6 is two times three, a number of the Goddess.

7 is the planets, time of the phases of the Moon, ways of Power.

8 is the Sabbats or festivals, and is a number of the God.

9 is the number of the Goddess, being three times three.

13 is the sign of the Coven; months of the Moon.

21 is the number of Sabbats and Esbats in the Wiccan year.

40 is a magical number used in charms.

101 is the number of fertility.

The planets are numbered thus:

Saturn, 3

Jupiter, 4

Mars, 5

Sun, 6

Venus, 7

Mercury, 8

Moon, 9

Rune Magic

Runes are symbols that, when drawn, painted, traced, carved, or visualized, release specific energies. As such, rune magic is surprisingly easy to practice and is undergoing a renaissance today.

In earlier times, runes were scratched onto birch bark, bone, or wood. They were carved onto weapons to ensure accurate shots, engraved on cups and goblets to ward off poisoning, and marked on goods and the home for protective purposes.

But much confusion surrounds these figures. Some feel that runes themselves contain hidden powers. The same is also said of the pentagram and other magical symbols. The thought here is that, simply by drawing a rune, the magician unleashes supernatural powers.

This isn't the case. Runes are tools of magic. *Their potency lies within their user.* If my neighbor happened to doodle a healing rune on a napkin and later used this to wipe his forehead, no healing energy would be transferred to him simply because he didn't put any into the rune.

Runes must be used with power to be magically effective. Carve, paint, or trace away—with visualization and with personal energy.

The ways to use runes are limited only by your imagination. For example, if a friend had asked me to speed her recovery from an illness, I might draw a healing rune on a plain piece of paper and sit before it. While concentrating on the rune, I'd visualize my friend in a healed, whole state. Then, after building up personal power, I'd send the energy to her *in the shape of the rune.* I'd see it meshing with her body, unblocking, soothing, healing.

Or, I could carve the rune on a piece of cedar wood, again visualizing perfect health, and give it to her to wear.

Runes can also be fashioned onto food—with power—and then eaten to bring that specific energy back into the body; marked on the person with oil and visualization; carved onto a candle that is then burned to release its energies; or traced or visualized in a pond or bathtub prior to entering it.

To draw runes on paper, specific ink colors related to each of the runes presented here can be found in their descriptions below, and can be utilized, if you wish. The colors work in harmony with the runes.

Excerpted from Wicca: A Guide for the Solitary Practitioner *by Scott Cunningham*

Good Fortune

This is a good, all-purpose rune, often used to close correspondence or engraved on jewelry.

Victory

Used in legal battles, and in general-purpose magic. Draw in scarlet ink, burn during ceremony or carry with you.

Love

This is used not only to receive and strengthen love, but also to send love to a friend. Draw with emerald green ink.

Comfort

To bring relief and ease, and to send or induce happiness and comfort. Draw in green for letters, talismans, etc.

Wealth

Draw in purple ink. It can be used in petitions, drawn on your business cards, etc. Its old name is Gilch.

GOOD FORTUNE

This is a good all-purpose rune, often used to close correspondence or engraved on jewelry.

VICTORY

Used in legal battles, and in general-purpose magic. Draw in scarlet ink, burn during ceremony or carry with you.

LOVE

This is used not only to receive and strengthen love, but also to send love to a friend. Draw with emerald green ink.

COMFORT

To bring relief and ease, and to send or induce happiness and comfort. Draw in green or letters, talismans, etc.

WEALTH

Draw in purple ink. It can be used in petitions, drawn on your business cards, etc. It's old name is Gilch.

Possession

This rune represents tangible objects. Draw in purple or green ink. Also known as "Ogal."

Disordered Thoughts

Burn to confuse one who would do you harm. Yellow ink. Also, visualize this rune on the person's head, or inside it.

War

To use in, or to stop or start, battles and conflicts. To stop one, draw in red ink, then completely blot out with white or pink ink or paint. Or, visualize the rune and smash it, then see it exploding, ceasing to be.

Man

To represent a man. Red ink.

Woman

To represent a woman. Green ink.

POSSESSION

This rune represents tangible objects. Draw in purple or green ink. Also known as "Ogal."

DISORDERED THOUGHTS

Burn to confuse one who would do you harm. Yellow ink. Also, visualize this rune on the person's head, or inside it.

WAR

To use in, or to stop or start battles and conflicts. stop one, draw in red ink, then completely blot out with or pink ink or paint. Or, visualize the rune and smash i see it exploding, ceasing to be.

MAN

To represent a man. Red ink.

WOMAN

To represent a woman. Green ink.

Friendship between two men, or brothers.

Friendship between two women, or sisters.

Friendship between man and woman.

Sexual activity between two men. Red ink.

Sexual activity between two women. Green ink.

Sexual activity between man and woman.

Friendship between two men, or brothers.

Friendship between two women, or sisters.

Friendship between man and woman.

Sexual activity between two men. Red ink.

Sexual activity between two women. Green ink.

Sexual activity between man and woman.

Rain

Draw this in blue ink on white paper. Use it during rain rituals outside. Let rain fall on it, and use next time as well. Can be used over and over.

Various protective runes to paint, astrally charge, or engrave on objects.

For the blessings of the Goddess. Silver ink.

For the blessings of the God. Gold ink.

Note: Runes may be visualized on any person or object; astrally drawn using the athame, wand, a finger, or with your mind; or drawn with anointing oil on a person, or on oneself, or on an object.

RAIN

Draw this in blue ink on white paper. Use it during rain
rituals outside. Let rain fall on it, and use next time as well.
Can be used over and over.

Various protective runes to paint, astrally charge, or engrave
on objects.

For the blessings of the Goddess. Silver Ink.

For the blessings of the God. Gold Ink.

Note: Runes may be visualized on any person or
object; astrally drawn using the athame, wand,
a finger or with your mind; or drawn with anointing
oil on a person or on oneself or an object.

Runic Alphabet

A	ᚨ
B	ᛒ
C	ᚲ
D	ᛞ
E	ᛖ
F	ᚠ
G	ᚷ
H	ᚺ
I	ᛁ
J	ᛃ
K	ᚲ
L	ᛚ
M	ᛗ
N	ᚾ
NG	ᛜ
O	ᛟ
P	ᛈ
Q	ᛩ
R	ᚱ
S	ᛊ
T	ᛏ
TH	ᚦ
U	ᚢ
V	ᚡ
W	ᚹ
X	ᚼ
Y	ᛦ
Z	ᛉ

RUNIC ALPHABET

Signs and Symbols

Symbols & Signs

- The Goddess
- The God
- Goddess Position
- God Position
- Great Rite (NOTE: NO LONGER USED)
- The Cup
- Cord
- Censer
- Pentacle
- Broom
- Wand
- Balefire
- Cauldron
- Altar
- Portal
- Waxing Moon
- Full Moon
- Waning Moon
- Dark; New Moon
- Sword
- Athamé
- Immortality
- Sunrise
- Sunset
- Magic Circle
- Candle
- Salt
- Herb
- Deadly, Bane, Poisonous
- Deosil
- Widdershins
- Water
- Wine

- North
- East
- South
- West
- Moonrise
- Moonset
- First Admission
- Second Admission
- Third Admission

Symbols are an important part of many Wiccan traditions. They're used as magical shorthand in the Book of Shadows; as a graphic representation of Wicca or a specific Wiccan tradition (on correspondence, perhaps); and to empower magical tools and jewelry.

The first ritual symbols used in Wicca stemmed largely from ceremonial magic (particularly those found in *The Key of Solomon*; see bibliography) and alchemy. Their number soon increased and became more specifically Wiccan, such as symbols for levels of initiation, the Circle, the Goddess, and the God. Traditions shared symbols among their adherents. They began to be published, further widening their usage.

Your tradition should probably utilize some symbols. Symbols (which are, in a sense, a compact alphabet) trigger powerful psychological responses, if their observer is aware of their meanings, because they speak to the subconscious mind.

You can create your own symbols or choose ones from those lists given below. I have only one warning: never use an unfamiliar symbol. If you don't know a symbol's meaning, it's best not to utilize it in any way.

Excerpted from Living Wicca: A Further Guide for the Solitary Practitioner *by Scott Cunningham*

The Goddess

The God

Goddess Position

)O(the Goddess

☿ the God

✗ Goddess Position

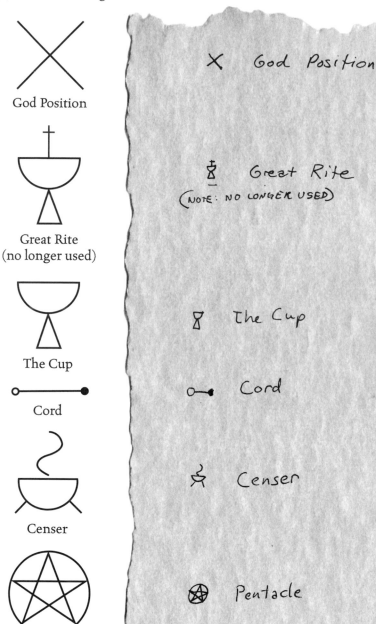

God Position

Great Rite
(no longer used)

The Cup

Cord

Censer

Pentacle

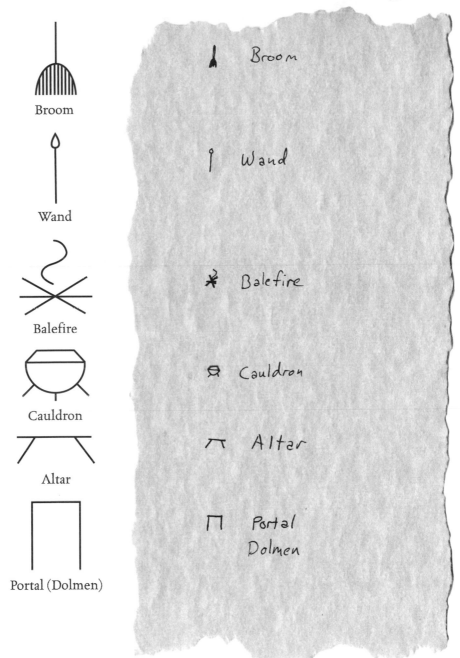

Broom

Wand

Balefire

Cauldron

Altar

Portal (Dolmen)

* Waning Moon

Full Moon

* Waxing Moon

Dark; New Moon

Sword

Athame

Immortality

Sunrise

* Editorial note: In this early work of Scott Cunningham's, the symbols for waxing and waning moons in his hand-drawn version were reversed. The printed illustration above shows the correct positions of the moons.

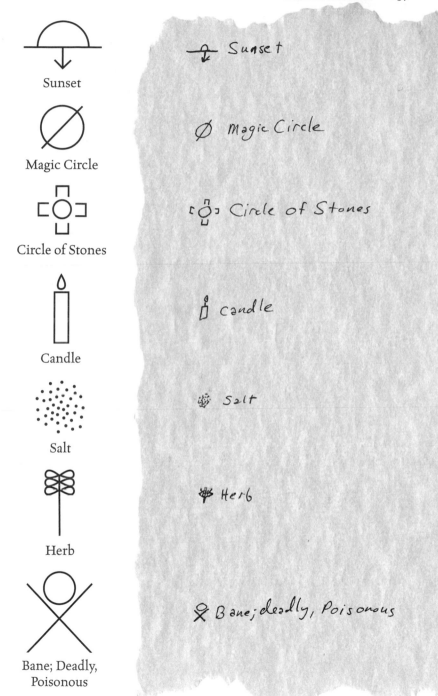

Sunset

Magic Circle

Circle of Stones

Candle

Salt

Herb

Bane; Deadly,
Poisonous

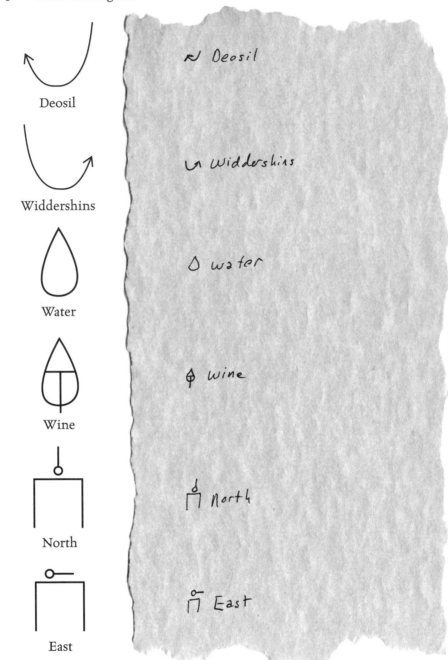

Deosil

Widdershins

Water

Wine

North

East

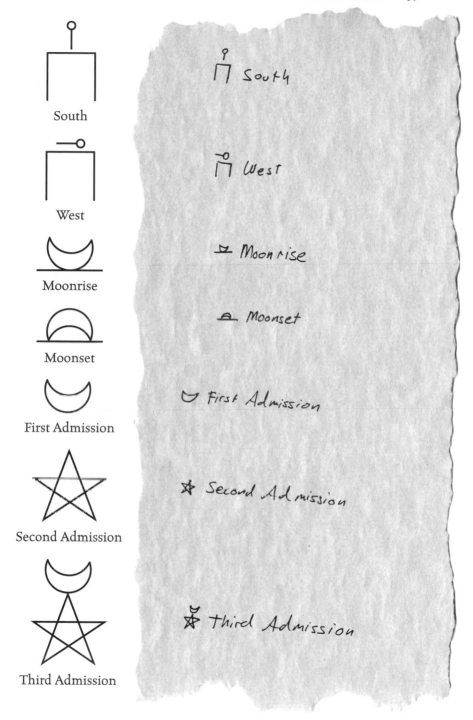

South

West

Moonrise

Moonset

First Admission

Second Admission

Third Admission

South

West

Moonrise

Moonset

First Admission

Second Admission

Third Admission

BIBLIOGRAPHY

This is a wide-ranging list of books related, in some way, to Wicca. A book's inclusion here doesn't necessarily indicate that I'm in perfect agreement with its contents. Many of these books were written from far different perspectives than the one you've been reading.

All, however, if read with intelligence and discrimination, will deepen your understanding of the Goddess and God, and of the myriad forms of Wicca, magic, and shamanism.

Those asterisked (*) are highly recommended.

Where I felt it important, I have appended short comments concerning the book's contents, *not* my views on them.

Such a list as this cannot hope to be complete. Books on these subjects are being published every day. Still, this should serve as a starting point for those interested in reading further.

Editor's note: This bibliography appeared in Scott Cunningham's *Wicca: A Guide for the Solitary Practitioner* (Llewellyn, 1988). It is reprinted here for the reader's convenience.

Shamanism

Andrews, Lynn V. *Medicine Woman*. San Francisco: Harper & Row, 1981.

Bend, Cynthia, and Tayja Wiger. *Birth of a Modern Shaman*. St. Paul: Llewellyn Publications, 1988.

Castaneda, Carlos. *The Teachings of Don Juan: A Yaqui Way of Knowledge*. New York: Ballantine, 1970.

Furst, Peter T. *Hallucinogens and Culture*. Corte Madera, CA: Chandler & Sharp Publishers, 1976.

*Harner, Michael J. (editor). *Hallucinogens and Shamanism*. New York: Oxford University Press, 1978.

*Harner, Michael. *The Way of the Shaman*. San Francisco: Harper & Row, 1981. The first how-to book on this subject, *The Way of the Shaman* introduces simple techniques for acquiring alternate states of consciousness, on contacting your power animal, healing rituals, and much else of interest.

*Howells, William. *The Heathens: Primitive Man and His Religions*. Garden City (New York): Doubleday, 1956. Covers the entire range of pre-Christian and pre-technological religion and magic, including totemism, ancestor worship, shamanism, divination, mana, and tabu.

Kilpatrick, Jack Frederick, and Anna Gritts. *Notebook of a Cherokee Shaman.* Washington DC: Smithsonian, 1970.

Lame Deer, John (Fire), and Richard Erdoes. *Lame Deer: Seeker of Visions.* New York: Pocket Books, 1978. A portrait of a contemporary shaman, revealing the essential humanness of the subject. Much Sioux lore.

Lewis, I. M. *Ecstatic Religion: An Anthropological Study of Spirit Possession and Shamanism.* Baltimore: Penquin, 1976. This is a scholarly sociological investigation into shamanism and alternate states of consciousness.

Rogers, Spencer L. *The Shaman's Healing Way.* Ramona, CA: Acoma Books, 1976.

*Sharon, Douglas. *Wizard of the Four Winds: A Shaman's Story.* New York: The Free Press, 1978. A portrait of Eduardo Calderon, a contemporary Peruvian shaman, detailing much of his rites and rituals.

*Torrey, E. Fuller. *The Mind Game: Witchdoctors and Psychiatrists.* New York: Bantam, 1973.

*Wellman, Alice. *Spirit Magic.* New York: Berkeley, 1973. This short paperback is a guide to shamanism as practiced in various parts of the world. One chapter, "The Tools of Wizardry," is of particular interest.

Goddess Studies

Briffault, Robert. *The Mothers.* (Abridged by Gordon Taylor.) New York: Atheneum, 1977.

Downing, Christine. *The Goddess: Mythological Images of the Feminine.* New York: Crossroad, 1984.

*Graves, Robert. *The White Goddess.* New York: Farrar, Straus and Giroux, 1973. Perhaps the book that has had the greatest effect on modern Wicca. A poetic investigation into the Goddess.

*Harding, Esther. *Women's Mysteries: Ancient and Modern.* New York: Pantheon, 1955.

James, E. O. *The Cult of the Mother-Goddess.* New York: Barnes and Noble, 1959.

Leland, Charles G. *Aradia, or the Gospel of the Witches.* New York: Buckland Museum, 1968. This work presents a very different view of the Goddess than most others. The material was collected by Mr. Leland in the late 1800s and has had an effect on current Wicca.

*Newmann, Erich. *The Great Mother: an Analysis of the Archetype.* Princeton: Princeton University Press, 1974. A Jungian approach to the Goddess. This book concludes with 185 pages of photographs of Goddess images.

Stone, Merlin. *When God Was a Woman.* New York: Dial Press, 1976.

Walker, Barbara. *The Women's Encyclopedia of Myths and Mysteries.* San Francisco: Harper & Row, 1983.

Folklore, Mythology, Legend and History

*Bord, Janet, and Colin Bord. *Earth Rites: Fertility Practices in Pre-Industrial Britain.* London: Granada, 1982. An account of pagan rituals of Britain.

Busenbark, Ernest. *Symbols, Sex and the Stars in Popular Beliefs.* New York: Truth Seeker, 1949.

*Campbell, Joseph. *The Masks of God: Creative Mythology.* New York: Viking Press, 1971.

———. *The Masks of God: Oriental Mythology.* New York: Viking Press, 1977.

———. *The Masks of God: Primitive Mythology.* New York: Viking Press, 1977. These books cover the whole sweep of worldwide mythology.

———. *Myths to Live By.* New York: Bantam Books, 1973.

*Carpenter, Edward. *Pagan and Christian Creeds: Their Origin and Meaning.* New York: Harcourt, Brace and Company, 1920. An early work by a renegade scholar, it shows the origins of many Christian religious symbols from earlier pagan religions. Along the way it covers food and vegetation magic, pagan initiations, ritual dancing, the sex-taboo, and much else of interest.

*Dexter, T. F. G. *Fire Worship in Britain.* London: Watts and Co., 1931. A forty-three-page booklet, printed before World War II, detailing the survival of ancient pagan festivals in Britain before that conflict ended many of them forever.

*Ehrenreich, Barbara, and Deirdre English. *Witches, Midwives and Nurses: A History of Women Healers.* Old Westbury, NY: 1973. An important investigation of the role of women as healers and witches in earlier times.

Evans-Wentz, W. Y. *The Fairy-Faith in Celtic Countries.* London: Oxford University Press, 1911. Gerrards Cross (Buckinghamshire, England): 1981.

Frazer, Sir James. *The Golden Bough.* New York: Macmillan, 1956. (One volume abridged edition.)

Harley, Timothy. *Moon Lore.* Tokyo: Charles E. Tuttle Co., 1970.

Kenyon, Theda. *Witches Still Live.* New York: Washburn, 1929. An early collection of myths, legends, and tales of Witches and folk magicians.

*Leach, Maria, editor, and Jerome Fried, associate editor. *Funk and Wagnall's Standard Dictionary of Folklore, Mythology and Legend.* New York: Funk and Wagnall's, 1972. This classic, one-volume collection nearly sums up the totality of mythic information. Of great interest to Wiccans.

Watts, Alan. *The Two Hands of God: The Myths of Polarity.* New York: Coffier, 1978.

Wicca

Bowness, Charles. *The Witch's Gospel.* London: Robert Hale, 1979.

Buckland, Raymond. *Witchcraft . . . The Religion.* Bay Shore (New York): The Buckland Museum of Witchcraft and Magick, 1966. An early explication of Gardnerian Wicca.

Buczynski, Edmund M. *The Witchcraft Fact Book.* New York: Magickal Childe, n.d.

Crowther, Patricia. *Witch Blood! The Diary of a Witch High Priestess.* New York: House of Collectibles, 1974.

Deutch, Richard. *The Ecstatic Mother: Portrait of Maxine Sanders—Witch Queen.* London: Bachman and Turner, 1977. One of the key figures of the Alexandrian Wiccan tradition is explored in this work.

*Gardner, Gerald. *The Meaning of Witchcraft.* London: Aquarian Press, 1971. An historical look at Wicca.

———. *Witchcraft Today.* New York: Citadel, 1955. The first book written about contemporary Wicca details what has come to be termed Gardnerian Wicca.

*Glass, Justine. *Witchcraft: the Sixth Sense and Us.* North Hollywood: Wilshire, 1965.

Johns, June. *King of the Witches: The World of Alex Sanders.* New York: Coward McCann, 1969. Another investigation of Alexandrian Wicca and a biography of its founder.

Lady Sara. *Questions and Answers on Wicca Craft.* Wolf Creek (Oregon): Stonehenge Farm, 1974.

*Leek, Sybil. *The Complete Art of Witchcraft.* New York: World Publishing, 1971. This influential work describes an eclectic Wiccan tradition.

———. *Diary of a Witch.* New York: Prentice-Hall, 1968.

"Lugh." *Old George Pickingill and the Roots of Modern Witchcraft*. London: Wiccan Publications, 1982. Taray, 1984. This work purports to describe the historical background to the modern revival of Wicca by Gerald Gardner.

Martello, Leo L. *Witchcraft: the Old Religion*. Secaucus: University Books, 1974. An investigation into Sicilian Wicca.

Roberts, Susan. *Witches USA*. New York: Dell, 1971. This book, an investigation into Wicca by an outsider, created a storm of controversy when it was reprinted. It stands as an overview of part of the Wiccan scene circa 1970, and is no more flawed by inaccuracies than any other book included in this list.

Sanders, Alex. *The Alex Sanders Lectures*. New York: Magickal Childe, 1980. Another look at Alexandrian Wicca.

Sanders, Maxine. *Maxine the Witch Queen*. London: Star Books, 1976. Yet another look, this time autobiographical, at the founding and activities of Alexandrian Wicca.

*Valiente, Doreen. *An ABC of Witchcraft Past and Present*. New York: St. Martin's, 1973. A Gardnerian Wiccan's answer to earlier Witchcraft books, this is an encyclopedic look at British Wicca, folklore, and legend.

*———. *Where Witchcraft Lives*. London: Aquarian Press, 1962. An early look at British Wicca and Sussex folklore.

Practical Instructions

*Alan, Jim, and Selena Fox. *Circle Magic Songs*. Madison, WI: Circle Publications, 1977.

Buckland, Raymond. *The Tree: The Complete Book of Saxon Witchcraft*. New York: Weiser, 1974.

*———. *Buckland's Complete Book of Witchcraft*. St. Paul: Llewellyn Publications, 1985 and 2002. A course in Wicca, drawn from several traditions. Includes a section on solitary practitioners.

Budapest, Z. *The Feminist Book of Light and Shadows*. Venice, CA: Luna Publications, 1976. An influential, first book of feminist Wicca.

———. *The Holy Book of Women's Mysteries Part I*. Oakland, CA: The Susan B. Anthony coven #1, 1979. An expanded version of the above book. A second volume was also published.

Crowther, Patricia. *Lid Off the Cauldron: A Wicca Handbook*. London: Robert Hale, 1981. Another how-to book.

*Farrar, Janet and Stewart Farrar. *Eight Sabbats for Witches*. London: Robert Hale, 1981. These once-Alexandrian Wiccans have explored new territory, incorporating much Irish lore and deity-forms. This book also presents a unique look at the origins of the so-called Gardnerian Book of Shadows.

*————. *The Witches' Way: Principles, Rituals and Beliefs of Modern Witchcraft*. London: Robert Hale, 1984. Further revelations concerning Gardner's Book of Shadows and much practical information.

*Fitch, Ed. *Magical Rites From the Crystal Well*. St. Paul: Llewellyn Publications, 1984. A collection of neo-pagan rituals for every occasion.

K., Amber. *How to Organize a Coven or Magical Study Group*. Madison, WI: Circle Publications, 1983. Guidelines for doing just that.

*Slater, Herman (editor). *A Book of Pagan Rituals*. New York: Weiser, 1974. Another collection of rituals, this time drawn from the Pagan Way.

*Starhawk. *The Spiral Dance: A Rebirth of the Ancient Religion of the Great Goddess*. San Francisco: Harper and Row, 1979. It seems strange that it's been nearly ten years since this book was first published. It has had a tremendous impact on Wiccan groups and individuals. Definitely Goddess- and woman-oriented, it includes exercises for developing magical fluency and many rituals as well.

Valiente, Doreen. *Witchcraft for Tomorrow*. London: Robert Hale, 1978. Valiente's work, the first of the modern how-to-practice-Wicca books, contains a complete Book of Shadows, which she wrote just for publication, as well as several chapters covering various aspects of Wicca.

*Weinstein, Marion. *Earth Magic: A Dianic Book of Shadows*. New York: Earth Magic Productions, 1980. This is a Wiccan book like no other. It contains complete, explicit information on forming alignments with "all five aspects" of the deities, working with familiars, the tools, and much else of interest. An expanded version has been published.

Spell Books

Buckland, Raymond. *Practical Candleburning Rituals*. St. Paul: Llewellyn Publications, 1971.

*Chappel, Helen. *The Waxing Moon: A Gentle Guide to Magic*. New York: Links, 1974.

Dixon, Jo, and James Dixon. *The Color Book: Rituals, Charms and Enchant-ments*. Denver: Castle Rising, 1978.

Grammary, Ann. *The Witch's Workbook*. New York: Pocket, 1973.

Huson, Paul. *Mastering Witchcraft*. New York: Berkeley, 1971. An early book responsible, in part, for the tremendous interest in occult matters during the early 1970s. Little of its information bears much resemblance to Wicca, or to the type of magic Wiccans practice.

Lorde, Simon, and Clair Lorde. *The Wiccan Guide to Witches Ways*. New South Wales (Australia): K. J. Forrest, 1980.

Malbrough, Ray T. *Charms, Spells and Formulas for the Making and Use of Gris-Gris, Herb Candles, Doll Magick, Incenses, Oils and Powders to Gain Love, Protection, Prosperity, Luck and Prophetic Dreams*. St. Paul: Llewellyn, 1986. A collection of Cajun magic from Louisiana.

Paulsen, Kathryn. *Witches Potions and Spells*. Mount Vernon: Peter Pauper Press, 1971.

*Worth, Valerie. *The Crone's Book of Words*. St. Paul: Llewellyn Publications, 1971, 1986.

Magic Books

Agrippa, Henry Cornelius. *The Philosophy of Natural Magic*. Antwerp, 1531. Secaucus: University Books, 1974. This is the first of the three books mentioned in the next entry.

*————. *Three Books of Occult Philosophy*. London: 1651. London: Chthonios Books, 1986. This book constituted the bulk of magical information known in the sixteenth century. Stones, stars, herbs, incenses, sigils, and all manner of delights are to be found in this book. Recently reprinted in its entirety for the first time in three hundred years.

*Baneft, Francis. *The Magus, or Celestial Intelligencer, Being a Complete System of Occult Philosophy*. 1801. New Hyde Park (New York): University Books, 1967. Ceremonial (as opposed to natural) magic.

*Burland, C. A. *The Magical Arts: A Short History*. New York: Horizon Press, 1966. A history of folk magic.

Devine, M. V. *Brujeria: A Study of Mexican-American Folk-Magic*. St. Paul: Llewellyn Publications, 1982.

Fortune, Dion. *Psychic Self-Defence*. London: Aquarian, 1967.

*Howard, Michael. *The Magic of Runes*. New York: Weiser, 1980.

————. *The Runes and Other Magical Alphabets*. New York: Weiser, 1978.

Koch, Rudolph. *The Book of Signs*. New York: Dover, 1955. A book of signs, symbols, and runes.

Leland, Charles Godfrey. *Etruscan Magic and Occult Remedies*. New Hyde Park (New York): University Books, 1963.

————. *Gypsy Sorcery and Fortune-Telling*. New York: Dover, 1971.

Mathers, S. L. MacGregor (editor and translator). *The Key of Solomon the King*. New York: Weiser, 1972.

*Mickaharic, Draja. *Spiritual Cleansing: A Handbook of Psychic Protection*. York Beach (Maine): Weiser, 1982. Some of the magic in this work is shamanistic in tone and origin.

*Pepper, Elizabeth, and John Wilcox. *Witches All*. New York: Grosset and Dunlap, 1977. A collection of folk magic drawn from the popular (now defunct) Witches Almanac.

Pliny the Elder. *Natural History*. Cambridge: Harvard University Press, 1956.

Shah, Sayed Idries. *Oriental Magic*. New York: Philosophical Library, 1957.

————. *The Secret Lore of Magic*. New York: Citadel, 1970. Extracts from several Renaissance books of ceremonial magic.

————. *Occultism: Its Theory and Practice*. Castle Books. n.d.

Valiente, Doreen. *Natural Magic*. New York: St. Martin's Press, 1975.

*Weinstein, Marion. *Positive Magic: Occult Self-Help*. New York: Pocket Books, 1978. An introduction to magic. An expanded edition of this popular book has also been published.

APPENDIX I

deTraci Regula

In late 2008, Bill Krause called me from Llewellyn, asking if there were any materials from Scott that might make a good book. After all these years, Scott's works were still finding new audiences and there was an appetite for more of his works for a new generation of the magically inclined.

There were several things that came to my mind, but they evaded me in the many boxes, bookcases, and outdated file formats of the archives. My search was not as thorough as it could have been, mainly because confronting the loss of Scott is still something that is very painful for me to do. Bill was persistent in his requests, but it seemed like this project was coming to a halt.

Then, one evening, looking at the cover of "Whispers of the Moon" where I have it facing out on a shelf in a glassed-in lawyer's bookcase because the photo of Scott on the cover is my favorite, I realized that, years before, I had placed several notebooks and envelopes of Scott's materials on the same shelf behind it. It was all waiting inches away from where I do my own work, yet I had forgotten until that moment that I had it there. I lifted up the glass door and slid it back, and I reached at random for a tightly-packed manila envelope. On it, in the hand that I knew so well, was "The American Traditionalist Book of Shadows," adorned with a pentagram and the comment that this was the manuscript to be used for copying to send to his students. It was the core of Scott's correspondence course, which he had offered to students before his books were published—arguably the book of magic of a young wizard, drawn from his earliest experiences—the sort of thing you might expect a just-maturing Harry Potter to have created for his extracurricular classes in advanced magic for his peers. He was ardent in his belief that Wicca needed an American expression. He felt that the largely British-dominated magical scene was due for a shaking-up, one that embraced the seemingly more American qualities of equality, independence, and a less restrictive hierarchy—a Book of Shadows that emphasized a greener, more natural magic that could be practiced in a simple and sacred way by virtually anyone.

As I looked at the manuscript, I saw all of this as if through water, my vision blurred by tears catching in my eyelashes. The other works in various stages of completion that I had thought Bill might want to consider were very different from this, a complete, basic magical system which Scott had pored over with his usual obsessive care for detail and which drew directly from Scott's personal experiences of what was necessary for the young Wiccan to know. And, outside of a few friends and the students he had taken on in those brief years before his own success as an author made it very difficult for him to find the time to teach individually, it had never been seen by anyone. Some of it he had used as a jumping-off point for sections of *Wicca: A Guide for the Solitary Practitioner*, but by then he was refining his work for a much larger intended audience and taking into consideration the multiple demands of editors and various publishing needs. This document is pure from the source, just what he wanted and needed to say to the young mages of both sexes who sought him out for guidance and instruction.

May you use it wisely and well, with love for the divine, for the green earth, and for each other. As Scott would say at the end of his letters, bright blessings.

—deTraci Regula
April 2009

APPENDIX II

Marilee Bigelow

When Llewellyn asked me to submit a story or anecdote for this book, so many thoughts flew into my mind that I was filled with a myriad of emotions. One after another, pivotal points in both our lives spun by, but eventually one memory kept recurring.

The Story of Snap Dragon

Witches' faces beaming bright,
In the flickering fire's light.

As Scott and I sprinted across the parking lot in the dark, I glanced over my shoulder, just in time to see the sun peeking up over the rim of the earth, shooting bolts of red, gold, and orange into the pre-dawn sky.

Earlier in the day, I had been a guest on a local television show, and Scott had chosen to come with me. At that time Scott kept his metaphysical interests quite close to his chest, choosing to stay in the background whenever possible. Nevertheless, he often accompanied me on various personal appearances, and it was always a comfort to know that he was somewhere in the crowd lending his support.

However, today was our Hallows celebration, and Scott and I were on a quest. We were attempting to find an open liquor store to buy several large bottles of high-proof alcohol. I had decided to present the game of "Snap Dragon" at our event, and that required special supplies. This fire tradition was extremely popular many years ago, and was a yearly custom until it sadly started to die out, and was now almost forgotten. Scott and I were eager to revive the old practice, and bring it back to life.

Arriving home, we took a large plate and carefully covered it with raisins. Next we slowly poured the alcohol over the top, being careful to saturate each and every fruit. Then with a long match we lit the platter on fire. Suddenly, the entire room was cast in a warm glow from the flaming light; we had begun the spirited game of Snap Dragon.

Abruptly, we realized that this was not a challenge for the faint-hearted. The goal of Snap Dragon is to "snap" the fiery raisins out of the inferno and into your mouth without getting burned! Dubiously, we looked at each other, and then eyed the hot blaze before us; nonetheless, Scott and I were determined. We squared our shoulders, took a deep breath, and with faces askew, we crooked our fingers above the burning flames.

As our arms wildly flailed about in an attempt to pop the wayward "Dragons" harmlessly between our lips, the spectacle of each other gyrating, cavorting, and hopping around the table caused us both to dissolve into uncontrollable fits of laughter. It was only after Snap Dragon had finally died down that, still grinning, we were able to regain our composure.

We quickly realized that if this rite was to be accomplished safely and effectively with so many people, we needed not only to adhere to our preagreed security precautions, but also to establish some preliminary guidelines—one of which was to have participants flick the raisins one at a time into a small cup instead of their mouths. This would reduce the possibility of burns, and would also give us a "Dragon" count for the final "Flame-Off," which was scheduled for the end of the evening.

That night, as the lights were dimmed and the dish was lit, flickering blue sparks danced as they swept across the plain of raisins and alcohol, their colorful waves of light casting shadows on the walls around us. I gazed at the shining illuminated faces so eager with anticipation, our brave and courageous champions, their fingers poised, ready to begin, and it reminded me of our ancient and primeval fires of old. Needless to say, Snap Dragon was a huge success (with a minimum of aloe required, by the way) and played with great enthusiasm for many years to come.

Much later, after covering prone bodies and placing pillows under already-sleeping heads, Scott and I tiptoed out together to sit on the back porch. We had been up long before the "first light" of our sacred holiday, and in grateful appreciation, I poured each of us a glass of sherry (we had been taught by our teacher that this was the Witch's drink). We sat talking quietly, delighted and thankful that our plans had gone so well, and as we raised our glasses in a final toast, I glanced over my shoulder just in time to see the sun peeking over the rim of the earth.

This is just one of the many wonderful memories I have of my friend and High Priest, Scott Cunningham. It didn't matter what crazy scheme I came up with—Snap Dragon, Flour Game, or the Rite of Candle and Water, Scott was always a willing and enthusiastic accomplice, as I was with him. Thank you for allowing me to share this remembrance with you.

—Marilee Bigelow
April 26, 2009

*Please note: The author advises not attempting Snap Dragon without the proper safety precautions, supervision, and instruction.

APPENDIX III

Christine Ashworth

Scott was always a giver. Of Chet and Rosie Cunningham's three kids, Scott was the most thoughtful, the least self-oriented, typical of a middle child.

Scott was also the creative one. The sensitive one. The only one who kept up with the piano lessons, the only one to sing in the church choir with Mom. One of my strongest, earliest memories of Scott was when he recreated parts of *Pirates of the Caribbean* in our back yard, with a pirate's chest of gold and a mound of jewels, inspired by our first trip to Disneyland. I must have been four at the time, and thought he was magical. Scott also collected rocks and seashells. My dad built a cabinet for him with a dozen or so flat drawers, to keep the shells in. He loved the ocean and the forests with equal fervor.

My parents owned a cabin in the Laguna Mountains, and summers would find us there, where we would grow dusty and brown in the sun. The three of us kids would hunt for frogs and tiny fishes in the marshes, unaware of how far we'd rambled. Scott always knew the way back, and he always picked flowers for Mom.

We reveled in summer thunderstorms, hanging out on our army cots on the sleeping porch, the screened windows open to the elements. Summer nights were filled with so many stars the sky looked crowded. Tall Jeffrey pine trees stood silhouetted against the night sky, perfuming the air with vanilla. Going to the mountains was our family escape—we all took on other personas there. Scott spent hours studying the rocks and flowers, the trees, searching for arrowheads and other signs of Native Americans, immersing himself in the place. All of us sank into our own private worlds, seemingly so much closer up there in the mountains than down at home. And yet, we remained a family unit—playing card games and board games, doing puzzles at one of the many kitchen tables in the rustic, octagonal main structure of the cabin, building a fire and sipping cocoa.

Scott must have been fourteen or fifteen when he started putting together Christmas stockings for my parents. It surprised me—parents getting stockings—but he did it with such whimsy and charm. One of his gifts was seeing into people, divining what they would appreciate. He was an excellent gift giver. Once he realized the Anthurium was my mother's favorite flower, that's part of what he'd give her for Mother's Day and her birthday. Christmas, too. In hindsight, his thoughtfulness and protectiveness of my mother was very sweet.

The year I turned sixteen, for my birthday, Scott bought the two of us tickets to see A *Chorus Line* in Los Angeles. He drove us up and we so enjoyed bouncing around Hollywood (seedier in the seventies than it is now). He even took me to Capezio's, so I could get a couple pairs of pointe shoes. And the show? Outstanding. Mesmerizing. Absolutely breathtaking, and such a joy to share it with him. The ride home was filled with our chatter about the dancing and the songs.

Scott and I moved out of the family home the month I graduated high school, in January of 1978. We shared an apartment on Orange Avenue for eight or nine months. Newly in love, I was rarely there and when I was, Scott wasn't. We drifted apart as only roommates on separate schedules can drift.

When I married and moved to Los Angeles, Scott remained a part of my life. Phone calls, letters the old-fashioned way, and visits. For him, success. Book sales came, and then the book tours. In between times he'd retreat to Hawaii to recuperate and research. When I had a good job, I'd drop him a check in the mail—surely his writing couldn't be paying the bills—and he'd always call with a thank you. Visits home were fun—Scott and my husband Tom would trade quips and jokes that flew way over my parents' heads. I might catch the double entendre once out of a dozen times, and would finally give up and just watch them enjoy each other.

Then March of 1990 hit, and news of Scott's illness passed along from his tour of the East Coast. We found out just as I celebrated being three months' pregnant with my first son. My pregnancy became a joy to focus on, in those first months of uncertainty.

The terrifying turned into the mundane. Scott grew stronger again and wrote and traveled. We talked and laughed and grew closer than we had been. The baby was born and Scott kept a respectful distance, not quite sure what to do with such a little thing.

But the disease stole him away. He grew weaker, and angry at not having the time to finish everything he'd wanted to do. Before he finally moved home so my parents could take care of him, he invited friends over, and gave away many of his books and things to people he knew would want or need them, sharing that last bit of himself that he could. He moved into my childhood room, his big iron bedstead taking up most of the tiny space, around Thanksgiving in 1992. And when he died in March of 1993, he'd fallen into a coma early in the morning. My mother held his hand, was there at his side when he finally passed that afternoon.

I was once again three months' pregnant, this time with my second son. I missed the pagan gathering for him in San Diego—my parents didn't tell me about it. There wasn't another memorial ceremony, not one that the family had planned. So it was just the family scattering his ashes up in the hills behind the cabin in the Laguna Mountains. Fourteen years later, that seemed the appropriate place to scatter my mom's ashes as well.

My private grief and regret over the lack of a more public memorial service, to this day, still hits me hard. It didn't seem right or fair, but I wasn't in charge. I spent several afternoons, over the next few months, sitting on the sand and staring out over the ocean. Sometimes weeping, sometimes angry, but always in dialog with Scott. I'd hear his laughter in the wind and the waves, and the Scott I was communing with, the Scott I missed, was the brother from my childhood, from those drowsy summer afternoons in the meadow, over the hill, and around the mountain from the cabin.

Finally, though, I started reading. I must confess, I'd never read his books until after he died. He never really expected me to be interested, I suppose. And in reading those books, I saw and grew to know the man he'd become, a deeper version of who he'd been when we were in the mountains as kids. The same, only—more. My creative, sensitive brother had grown to be funnier. Smarter. Stronger. More compassionate, more tangible, more open, even while guarding his privacy. His heart and soul are in those books, a clear expression of his driving need to share what had taken him so much effort to learn. It shouldn't be that hard, he'd once told me. To find a different way to worship—and such a natural way—well, for those who want to, learning it shouldn't be such a difficult task.

Scott has always been good at giving. The sharing of his knowledge with the rest of us is his ultimate gift.

Blessings,
Christine Ashworth
Simi Valley, California
April 2009

APPENDIX IV

David Harrington

Scott had so much responsibility for his work that every once in a while, to relieve the stress and tension of work, he would do a project just for fun. He had never lost his childlike joy in games and toys, and he would employ his considerable creative powers in creating new entertainments. His love of fantasy was intense; he lived in it and it would come through in myriad ways, and one of these was the Witch Game. While this might be considered politically uncorrect in these days of "Wicca," it didn't feel that way then—instead it was a way of reclaiming the pejorative term of "Witch."

One day he brought it over, presenting it with great ceremony. And I asked him what it was, and he said "It's my Flying Witch game."

I went, "Where did you get it?"

"I made it."

We put the game down on the floor and opened it up, and I was surprised at the ornateness of it. He had put a lot of time into placing the pictures on the box, so it resembled other board games popular at the time. He had created the full board, the game box, and all of the game pieces. He made the witches using the caps from wide-tipped markers, gluing them on top. I was amazed. "How cool!" He laid it out to work on it, since it was a work in progress, and so we would play it constantly to work out the rules and order of play and to see how it would flow. He wanted to put the game on the market and he was very proud of it. Since I'm childish too, or childlike, I enjoyed it because it was something different. I knew that whatever Scott created would be something fun, and it was. And through this, he also trained me. He would talk to me about all the things he had on the board and how they related to witchcraft, because I was still a student, and this was a great way to teach me, but also in an entertaining way, as we moved our markers around the labyrinthine turns of the game's path. He never *taught* me—he would start talking, and I would listen, and that's how I learned. The game was about a flying and thus "traveling" witch and somehow, playing it helped us think of places we wanted to go for our own magical journeys.

We explored natural magic, deciding to go into the wild and study from nature, like the old ones did, rather than from books in living rooms. We got on well because I was the first one to willingly go out with him into the wild, hiking in Borrego Springs to dig fossils, or going to Hagstone Cove to find mermaid tears, or driving to the old mission of Santa Ysabel to experience the local Mexican folk rituals of the Day of the Dead.

The "Witch Game" was very "Harry Potter"-like. When I saw the Harry Potter movies, they reminded me of the Witch Game, particularly the Marauder's Map and some of the other magical objects. I think there is a resemblance to Scott in Harry Potter—his innocence, above all; even though he could be sharp and cutting, he always meant well. They share the same essential goodness. From my perspective, he was a leader of the groups he was in and nobody could top him, as far as I could see. He took charge like Harry Potter—not too willingly, or with a lot of ego, but simply because there were things that needed to be done and he knew how to do them, or could figure it all out. He was just so bright—and I think his precocity and warmth shines through in this early book of shadows.

—David Harrington
July 2009